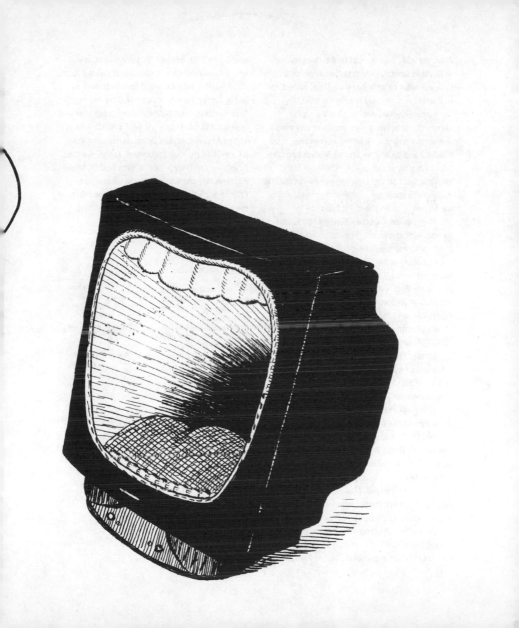

Above all, my gratitude to everyone at ESPN in Bristol, New York, Los Angeles and Bellevue who contributed their time, expertise and best lines. You are simply the best.

I owe a special debt to John Walsh for setting the standards high and coaching me to live up to them. Eric Schoenfeld kept me checked and balanced. Sharyn Taymor kept the trains running at full-speed. Howie Schwab kept the facts straight. Kil-Jae Hong kept the book in the spotlight. Thank you for welcoming me so warmly into the ESPN family.

At Hyperion, Gretchen Young's commitment to creativity and quality is a continual gift. It was a pleasure working closely with her, Jennifer Morgan and Jennifer Lang. Thanks also to Adrian James, Lesley Krauss, John Marius and Audra Zaccaro for taking such care with production and printing, Laurie Rippon and Tracey Menzies for marketing the book with style and enthusiasm and Robert Miller and Kris Kliemann for their ongoing support.

Charles Barkley proved that athletes can shine both on and off the court, while Steve Lefkowitz and Marc Perman proved that Jerry Maguire wasn't just a Hollywood creation.

This book rests on the quality – and quantity – of the quotes it contains, and I was blessed to have the very smart (and totally committed) Leslie Boghosian and John Carlin screening tapes on what was often a 24-hour basis, ably backed up by James Minnich and Jeff Rhode. Jenny Ford, Monica Schroer and Felicity Stone are the linchpins of the small, and versatile, ESPN Books editorial team. Thanks to Ben Shannon who enthusiastically chipped in at the last minute. I can't thank my fellow Canadian expatriates, Teresa Fernandes

and Barry Blitt, enough for their vision, talent and humor (and their son's love of Jaromir Jagr).

And, finally, a personal note of thanks to Betsy Carter, John Mack Carter, Gary Hoenig, Tom Hopkins, Paul Sullivan, Glen Waggoner and Tom Wolf for making me a better editor and Thalia Assuras, Blythe Bohonos, Susan Casey, Bruce Charlap, June Dickenson, Zsuzsi Gartner, Kathleen and Harvey Leach, John Lekich, Mary Ellen McMahon, Ann and Norm Richardson, Felicity Stone and Aleksi Suvanto for making me a better person. Yes, the two do overlap.

Shelley Youngblut

The Quotable ESPN © 1998
Hyperion/ESPN Books

Printed in the United States of America.

Library of Congress Cataloging-in-Publication Data

The Quotable ESPN
p. cm.
ISBN 0-7868-8291-3

1. Sports
2. ESPN (Television network)
3. American wit and humor

First Edition
10 9 8 7 6 5 4 3 2 1

Editorial Director
Shelley Youngblut

Designer
Teresa Fernandes

Associate Editors
Jenny Ford
Monica Schroer

Lead Researchers
Leslie Boghosian
John Carlin

Researchers
James Minnich
Jeff Rhode

Copy Editor
Felicity Stone

"Welcome to this **fine, quality** sports product."

"If you're a fan, what you'll see in the next minutes, hours, days to follow may convince you you've gone to sports heaven." Those were the first words heard on ESPN, back on September 7, 1979. Well, it's taken 19 years, but ESPN has called the ultimate sixth man in off the bench to have the last word. I like spicy things, to get discussions started, whether we're talking role models or racism, rookies or Rodman. I was chosen for some reason to live this life, and if all I do is make a lot of money and never speak out for anybody or myself, that would be a waste. I've said and done some things wrong, but I can honestly say I've been more right than wrong. Am I going to heaven? It's going to be a real close vote. –CHARLES BARKLEY

A Sir Charles Sampler

On being an athlete and a role model (*Up Close Primetime, 1997*):

"We all make mistakes. But anytime an athlete does something seriously wrong it hurts me, because we are a fraternity."

On being a 13-season NBA veteran (*Up Close, 1997*):

["Seemed like it was **yesterday** that **I could dunk**."]

On the downside of how the NBA markets itself (*Up Close Primetime, 1997*):

"The NBA makes everybody a star because they just want to make money. You got guys who can't even play that got jerseys, shoes and everything. There are probably three or four great players in the league. I don't feel like I'm there anymore, but I'm right below that."

On the difference between him and Dennis Rodman (*Up Close, 1997*):

"Dennis likes wearing a dress, I don't like wearing a dress. I tried it on a couple of times in the house but I do it privately, I don't do it publicly."

On racism (*Up Close*, *1994*):

"It's **really wrong** for black people **to be racists**,
because two wrongs don't make a right.
White people don't know any better,
that's the way they were taught, but
black people know how it feels."

On the secret to success (*Up Close*, *1997*):

"You can be **as successful**
as you want to be but you have to
push yourself and the only way to
do that is **through education**.
You **can't blame** your **Mom**, you
can't blame your **Dad**, you **can't
blame white people**, you **have** to
take control of your **own life** and
make yourself successful."

On the ups and downs of being in the spotlight (*Up Close*, *1997*):

"No matter how many things you do positive,
if you do one thing negative, you're done."

9

Over four score and seven years ago, great statesmen, famous politicians, obscure philosophers and your everyday athletes have been reciting verse worth repeating . . . and repeating . . . and repeating. . . . In fact, it appears that this love affair with pontificating is "not over till it's over." Many, if not all, TV sports shows feature a play of the day, of the week, of the year, of the decade. I'd like to offer up a new segment called "Say of the Day" because it seems athletes really do have something to say (although that may have something to do with the sea of microphones that's planted daily in their faces). So, repeat after me, some of the notable quotables. . . . –DAN PATRICK

"Dare I say, en fuego!"

Dan Patrick, after using his trademark "en fuego" to describe Ryan Smyth's hat trick in an Oilers win over the Maple Leafs (*SportsCenter, 1996*):

> ## "Yes, somebody left the ESPN cliché cabinet open and I went to town."

Bill Murray and **Tony Bennett**, revealing the lyrics to the *SportsCenter* theme (*ESPY Awards, 1994*):

"Oh my God, it's **that song** – that song that means *SportsCenter's* on! **My life can wait** – I've got a very important date. I can't walk the dog, feed the kids, take a bath, wash my hair, brush my teeth or take a job anytime I hear that '**da-da-da, da-da-da**.'"

Roger Staubach (*"The Ego Game," Outside the Lines, 1993*):

"Quarterbacks are like the tea bags of life. They've got to perform while the water's hot."

Steve Levy, on Allen Adams, who won a contest to kick a field goal during half-time of a Steelers-Ravens game, then was arrested on an outstanding warrant (*SportsCenter, 1996*):

"Bottom line: he **missed all three kicks**, then was **handcuffed** and **taken to jail**. How was your Sunday in comparison?"

Yogi Berra, giving advice to the graduating class of New Jersey's
Montclair State College (*SportsCenter*, 1996):

"As I once said, I really didn't say everything
I said, so now it's my turn. . . . During the years ahead,
when you come to the fork in the road, take it. . . .

Always follow the crowd, because nobody goes there.

It's too crowded. . . . Stay alert.
You can observe a lot by watching."

George Foreman, looking back at his role in the
Rumble in the Jungle (*Sunday Conversation*, 1995):

{ **"The Rope a Dope would not have existed without the Big Dope."** }

Martina Navratilova, on why she hates being referred to as
the lesbian tennis player (*Sunday Conversation*, 1993):

"They don't write Joe Montana, the heterosexual football player."

Deion Sanders (*Sunday Conversation*, 1995):

"I want to be the **first black dude** to have
a fishing show, *Fishing with Prime Time*."

13

Chris "Boomer" Berman, on the origin of his trademark nicknames (*Berman's Best: The Nickname Show, 1993*):

"Well, we have to **go back** to the Dark Ages: **the mid-'70s**, before they had cable. **I was at school** at Brown University and a group of us would sit around looking at **baseball box scores**. You had to **nickname the players**, all the while **sipping on our favorite beverage** – Perrier, of course."

Boxing writer **Bert Sugar** (*Berman's Best: The Nickname Show, 1993*):

{ "Every fighter's got to have a nickname. If you don't have a **nickname on the back of your robe** or if Michael Buffer cannot announce you with a nickname, you might as well go home. You're not **going to win**." }

Charles Barkley, on the difference between the WNBA and the NBA (*Up Close, 1997*):

"Our **best player** in Houston **is pregnant** – that **can't happen in the NBA**."

Houston Comets forward **Sheryl Swoopes**, on Michael Jordan's response when she asked him if she could name her son Jordan (*ESPN.SportsZone, 1997*):

"He rubbed my stomach and said, 'Only if he has a sweet jumper.'"

Keith Olbermann, reporting on the College Football Awards (*SportsCenter, 1996*):

"Florida quarterback Danny Wuerffel won **three trophies tonight –** the O'Brien, Maxwell and Smart Athlete. Combine the last two, and Danny won **the Maxwell Smart Award."**

John Kruk, on what it means to be a "throwback player" (*Sunday Conversation, 1992*):

> "**No one else wanted us. They threw us back into the pile and the Phillies had to take us. I think that's what it means.**"

Stuart Scott, on the G.I. Joe 200 (*SportsCenter, 1997*):

> "Those CART people understand the value of the lifelike hair and the kung-fu grip."

Barry Bonds, accepting the ESPY for Outstanding Male Athlete (*ESPY Awards, 1993*):

> "I'll probably **go down in history** for winning more awards **except for the one I want.**"

Dusty Baker, when asked about the Giants' prospects after going down 2-0 in their divisional series against the Marlins (*SportsCenter, 1997*):

> "It's not a must-win situation, it's a **have-to-win** situation."

Bristol University Dean, **Chris Berman**, instructing students in football rhetoric (*NFL Countdown commercial, 1997*):

"There is no such thing as a stupid question, just stupid people that ask questions."

Duke University coach, **Mike Krzyzewski**, on his team being upset by Providence in the second round of the NCAA tournament (*SportsCenter, 1997*):

"We didn't lose the game – we got beat by a team that was better than us."

Jim Harbaugh, on whether the pain of being a quarterback lessens over a season (*Up Close, 1997*):

"YOU'RE KIND OF NUMB AFTER 50 SHOTS TO THE HEAD."

Michael Jordan, on his biggest fear (*Up Close, 1989*):

"Snakes."

Dan Davis, updating a PGA tournament lead by David Peoples (*ESPN Radio Network, 1992*):

"Don't know how many pars Peter Persons posted, but Peter Persons must pick up the pace to press Peoples tomorrow."

David Letterman (*ESPY Awards, 1994*):

"I'm here to **present the ESPY** for **Auto Racing**. It's the kind of thing you have to do when you get **8 points against your license**."

Craig Kilborn, introducing a highlight featuring Trailblazer Arvydas Sabonis (*SportsCenter, 1996*):

"He's not my vydas, he's not your vydas, he's Arvydas."

Charley Steiner, on why boxing's scoring system makes it a more maddening sport to cover than college football (*ESPN Radio Network, 1997*):

"In **what other sport** is there a guy from **a country that you need an atlas to tell you where it is**, who has **a name you can barely pronounce**, who tells you with **his scorecard** that **you didn't see** what **you swore you saw?**"

Keith Olbermann, on Glen Rice averaging more than 35 points in five straight games *(SportsCenter, 1997)*:

"He's minute Rice, he's instant Rice, he's Rolls Rice."

Steve Levy *(SportsCenter, 1997)*:

> "Let's get ready to stumble. Can't say rumble, it's copyrighted."

Isiah Thomas *(Sunday Conversation, 1992)*:

"I've always wanted to be a Boston Celtic."

Dick Schaap, commenting upon Keyshawn Johnson's autobiography, *Give Me the Damn Ball!* *(The Sports Reporters, 1997)*:

"I can't wait until next year when Neil O'Donnell writes his book called *Catch the Damn Ball!*"

Kenny Mayne, coming up with a better Ken Griffey Jr. home-run call than "It's never iffy if it's Griffey" *(SportsCenter, 1997)*:

"I am amused by the simplicity of this game."

Wilt Chamberlain (*Up Close, 1981*):

"Bill Walton had a definite aroma about him."

Mitch Albom, on Barry Sanders (*NFL Prime Monday, 1996*):

"The **biggest misuse of talent**
since Tom Hanks in ***Bosom Buddies***. He's
a **half-open Christmas present**."

Karl Malone, on the proliferation of entourages in the NBA (*Up Close Primetime, 1997*):

> "Some guys can't function without four or five guys in their car. Some guys can't function without a guy going and ordering a burger for them. I'm from Louisiana. Excuse me, but we're used to doing things ourselves."

Charles Barkley, on the pervasiveness of beepers in the NBA (*Up Close Primetime, 1997*):

"Unless you're a doctor, ain't nothing important they can't wait to call you about later. How many 19- or 20-year-old kids got something really important happening? We've had beepers go off in the middle of meetings right before the game."

Dan Patrick and **Bill Murray**, ribbing Michael Jordan about winning the ESPY for Comeback Athlete of the Year (*ESPY Awards, 1996*):

"You were in the minor leagues last year in Birmingham, which is a tough gig. But this Monica Seles girl was in the hospital, Mike!"

A foreign journalist, questioning Karl Malone at the Atlanta Olympics (*SportsCenter, 1996*):

"I'm from Denmark and I'm kind of **new in this business**. I just want to know **why you get two points** every time you **score**?"

Karl Malone's response:

"That's a **tough** question. **I thought I'd heard them all**. These are **just the rules** of the game, my man. You get two points – **don't try to change it**."

Kenny Mayne, on the U.S. drawing Iran as its opponent in Game 2 of the 1998 World Cup (*SportsCenter, 1997*):

"No doubt signmakers in Iran are busy drawing up placards reading, Defeat the Great Satan. It's safe to say we won't be able to count on the Iranian parents to bring orange slices for our players at halftime."

Linda Cohn, reporting on the Rangers' 8-11-8 start to the 1997-98 season (*SportsCenter, 1997*):

"The Rangers continue to suffer from PMS – Post Messier Syndrome."

Frank Deford (*ESPN Radio Network, 1997*):

"Who do you think the New York City Council's Black and Hispanic Caucus has voted as the most cherished African-American celebrity in all of America today? Give up? The answer is Don King. And I'm the King of Siam."

ESPY host **Dennis Miller**, in his opening monologue (*ESPY Awards, 1994*):

"Right now, there are a **thousand** guys in Alabama looking at me, saying, **'Hey, that's not *Speed Week.*'**"

Rick Pitino, on Dino Radja refusing to report to the Sixers after being traded by the Celtics (*SportsCenter, 1997*):

> "He said he'd like to go to a warm climate and a contender. We explained to him that it's not a Club Med."

Jim Kelly, on which Bills game tapes he'd want his children to see (*Sunday Conversation, 1994*):

"One thing I know for sure, they won't see any of the Super Bowl games."

Wayne Gretzky, on his superstitions (*Up Close*, *1994*):

"I don't like my hockey sticks **touching other sticks**, and I don't like them **crossing one another**, and I kind of have them **hidden in the corner**. I put **baby powder** on the ends. I think it's essentially **a matter of taking care** of **what takes care of you.**"

Jerry Rice, on why he shines his helmet and wears a new pair of shoes for every game (*Up Close*, *1996*):

"To **play good** you have to **look good.**"

Nick Bakay, on the absurdity of the NFL's quarterback rating system (*NFL Countdown*, *1997*):

"The system reads like the owner's manual to an Iranian boom box."

Michael Jordan, to Bulls fans after winning his first championship (*SportsCenter*, *1992*):

"Thank God **you** drafted me **instead** of **Portland**."

Phil Jackson, on sports talk radio ("*Sports Talk Mania*," *Outside the Lines*, *1995*):

"I listen to National Public Radio. I'd rather be informed than misinformed."

Chris Myers, describing a Chico Lind home run (*Baseball Tonight*, 1993):

"It's a Rush Limbaugh shot – way right, but still fair."

Kenny Mayne, reporting that Firecrest had bumped Silver Charm during the Belmont Stakes warm-ups (*SportsCenter*, 1997):

"A horse is a horse of course, of course, and no one can talk to a horse of course, but if we could, we would say to an animal named Firecrest, What is wrong with you? There's a Triple Crown title on the line, and you nearly screwed up the whole thing."

NFL agent **Drew Rosenhaus**, on the role of the sports agent (*Up Close Primetime*, 1996):

"Without us, the player and the team can't exist. We're the buffer. We keep this engine moving smoothly. We're the oil, so to speak."

Charley Steiner (*ESPN Radio Network*, 1997):

"Mike Tyson's wife gave birth to a baby boy. My suspicion is that in the Tyson household teething will be encouraged."

Sonics coach **George Karl** (*Up Close, 1997*):

"**Young players** only care about the **highlight reels,** endorsement **contracts** and **rap albums.** They are more interested in **what their agent** says than **what their coach** says."

Rich Eisen, of Disney-owned ESPN, reporting that Pierre Page might be named the next coach of the Disney-owned Mighty Ducks of Anaheim (*SportsCenter, 1997*):

"Pierre, just in case you're wondering, our **dental plan** is fabulous."

Wade Boggs, on the difference between playing in Boston and New York (*Sunday Conversation, 1994*):

"**New York's** more **laid back**."

Dan Patrick (*ESPN.SportsZone, 1996*):

"Our **anchors** are some of the **worst athletes** in the history of mankind. I get **teary-eyed** just thinking about how **pathetic** these guys are. The **best** athlete in the building? **Robin Roberts**."

Kevin Mitchell, on what Willie Mays said to him after his famous
bare-handed catch (*Sunday Conversation, 1992*):

"I **didn't teach** you that.
Catch the ball with **your glove**."

Richard Nixon (*Sunday Conversation, 1992*):

"Politics is just a great sport when you really put it in
its lowest common denominator."

Jimmy Roberts, on fraudulent baseball autographs
(*"The Autograph Game," Outside the Lines, 1990*):

"Used to be you'd make a **mistake** and
it'd break your heart. Nowadays,
it'll break your bank."

Dan Patrick, on the hardest part of his job (*ESPN.SportsZone, 1996*):

"**Admitting** to yourself you're
wearing makeup."

Tom Glavine, on choosing to pursue professional baseball
over hockey (*Sunday Conversation, 1996*):

"I had all my own teeth and
I wanted to keep it that way."

Sparky Anderson, on who should replace Bud Selig
(*ESPN.SportsZone, 1997*):

{ "If I had my choice, it would be a former baseball star. Does a lawyer know what a doctor does? Does a plumber know what a doctor does? If you haven't been down there, you don't know what it is like down in the pit." }

Dick Schaap (*The Sports Reporters, 1992*):

"Remember, if we sound stupid, it's not your television set, we are stupid."

Dolphins receiver **Lamar Thomas,** on what Dan Marino is saying when
he yells at his receivers (*The NFL on ESPN Radio, 1997*):

**"Get more open –
I'm getting old."**

Beano Cook (*SportsCenter, 1987*):

"You only have to bat **1.000** in two things —
flying and **heart transplants**. Everything
else you can go **four** for **five**."

Michael Irvin, on the upside of being in the media
spotlight (*Sunday Conversation, 1992*):

"You get the SUNDAY CONVERSATIONS."

Astro **Craig Biggio**, on the clichés involved in "getting it done" (*ESPN Radio Network, 1997*):

"Hey, you respect **the game**. You're not bigger than the game – you respect it, **appreciate the uniform**, every day you get the opportunity to come put it on you go out and **give it 100 percent**. I mean, **that's all you can ask for** – you go out there and you **give it your all**. If you're good, you're good that day; if you're bad, you're bad. But as long as you give it 100 percent, that's all you can ask. But respect it and **go about your business** – just do your job and execute and do what you have to do and **stay within your own abilities**; don't try to do more than you're capable of doing – **doing your job and staying healthy**. If you can stay healthy, hopefully you can do something. As far as that is, **I'm just trying to stay healthy, go about my business and win**. The only thing I'm concerned about is **winning ball games** and **getting to the next level.**"

29

Peter Gammons's top 10 reasons players missed starts since Cal Ripken Jr.'s streak began (*SportsCenter, 1995*):

10. Rickey Henderson: sidelined with frostbite after leaving **ice pack** on his foot.

9. Kevin Mitchell: missed a week with a pulled rib cage muscle after **vomiting.**

8. Dave Nilsson: sidelined with a strain of malaria after getting a **mosquito bite.**

7. John Smiley: slammed a **car door** on his hand.

6. Bob Ojeda: missed starts when **stung by a bee; fell** into **a bathtub; sliced his finger** trimming a hedge.

5. Dennis Martinez: strained shoulder **tossing a suitcase** on an equipment truck.

4. Jack Clark: asked out of lineup **due to stress** from an estimated $10-million debt including 18 luxury cars

3. Dwight Gooden: **hit by golf club** swung in the Mets clubhouse by Vince Coleman.

2. Pascual Perez: could not find exit off Atlanta beltway and **circled city** for four hours.

1. Chris Brown: missed a game with a **strained eyelid** after he slept on it wrong.

Strike!

ESPY host **John Goodman**, in his opening monologue (*ESPY Awards, 1995*):

"How many of you get the feeling that there's a professional host out there on strike and I'm just a replacement host?"

John Kruk, accepting the ESPY for Best Entertainment Performance by an Athlete (*ESPY Awards, 1995*):

"Everyone's been getting up here and thanking their teammates. I'm a free agent – I have none. So the hell with you, too."

Dan Patrick, on the ratification of the baseball labor deal (*SportsCenter, 1996*):
"Just in time for the holidays, baseball's labor peace on earth and good will to all men."

CHAPTER 2

We hear it all the time. "Boy, you have a great job. I wish I could be a sportscaster." Most of the time, it is an enviable gig. But then there are those intense post-game moments when an athlete has just poured hours of emotion and sweat on to the field and we (in our barely creased suits and ties) must walk into their locker room (their office), stick a microphone in their drained faces and ask the most loathed three-letter word in sports: How? How did you pull off that win? How does it feel to lose? Tough questions to ask. Even tougher ones to answer. –MIKE TIRICO

Pat Riley (*Sunday Conversation, 1992*):

"I believe there is **winning** and **misery**, and even when we win **I'm miserable.**"

Skier **A.J. Kitt** (*"Winning and Losing," Outside the Lines, 1993*):

"Winning is the only thing there is. Anything below first is losing. I'm not satisfied with anything but first; second and third are consolations, and fourth sucks."

Jim Valvano, on his reaction when N.C. State won the 1983 NCAA Championship (*Up Close, 1984*):

"All the **other coaches** win the national championship, they button their coat, they go **shake hands** with their opponent. **This guy goes out of his tree**. Why? Because all my life I had grown up **watching *Wide World of Sports***. Remember what the **agony of defeat** was? The skier. But the **joy of victory**, they don't have one. **I was going to give 'em one.**"

Dan Patrick, on what will happen if Dick Trickle ever wins
the Winston Cup (*ESPN.SportsZone, 1997*):

"It will be a national holiday at ESPN."

Joe Paterno (*Sports Look, 1980s*):

> "I **get a kick** out of people saying,
> You're **winning ugly**. I think you
> **end with** the word **win.**"

Rockets coach **Rudy Tomjanovich** (*"Winning and Losing," Outside the Lines, 1993*):

"When you're winning, it could be a cloudy day and you still feel good, the food tastes better, the travel's not as bad and your wife looks better."

Jeff Gordon, on his 1996 victory lane phone call to owner
Rick Hendrick (*Sunday Conversation, 1997*):

"I grabbed the phone and I'm screaming,
We won the Daytona 500!, and I shut the
engine off and he's like, **Who is this?**"

Jack Nicklaus, on winning his sixth Masters (*SportsCenter, 1986*):

"I don't know if I'll ever do it again or not, but frankly I don't really care."

Announcer **Al Michaels**, on coining "Do you believe in miracles?" as the U.S.A. hockey team defeated the Soviet Union to win the 1980 gold medal (*Up Close, 1986*):

"All I kept thinking to myself in the **final minute** of the game was, **Don't say anything stupid**, because you are going to have to live with yourself and **this is major** as far as **sporting history** is concerned. So whatever you say, **try to make it good**."

Former NASCAR champion **Benny Parsons** (ESPN.*SportsZone, 1997*):

"A race car driver's resume needs to say one thing: **winner**."

Wildcat **Gary McLain**, on Villanova's upset of Georgetown
in the NCAA Tournament (*SportsCenter, 1985*):

**"This is the best feeling in
the world. You can't buy it,
you can't even go to
Fantasy Island to get it."**

Magic Johnson (*Up Close, 1997*):

"I want to be successful and I want to win.
It's not just on the basketball court, it's checkers,
it's softball, it's basketball, just playing with my
son or sister – it doesn't matter."

Jimmy Johnson, on becoming coach of the Dolphins (*Up Close, 1996*):

**"I could b.s. you and tell you I want to
win a Super Bowl to get Dan Marino his
first ring. But the truth is I want to
do it for Jimmy Johnson much more
than I want to do it for Dan Marino."**

Sugar Ray Leonard (*Up Close, 1987*):

"I don't believe in **praying for a victory**.
I pray that **no one gets hurt**."

Joe Torre (*Up Close Primetime, 1997*):

"If **we lose** the game, I can **sleep ten hours** and I'd **be tired** when I get up. If **we win** a game, I could **sleep three hours** and I'm **wide awake**."

Allen Iverson (*Sunday Conversation, 1997*):

"I'd **rather win** than have **good sportsmanship**."

Jerome Bettis, on bowling a perfect 300 game (*NFL Prime Monday, 1996*):

"It was probably the **biggest accomplishment** of my life."

Troy Aikman (*Up Close Primetime, 1997*):

"Ultimately, as a quarterback, it's not numbers that we're judged on, it's how many championships you can win. I've always said Jerry Jones is not paying me to go out and throw for 4,000 yards. He pays me to win football games for him."

Kirk Gibson, after the Dodgers won the 1988 World Series (*SportsCenter, 1988*):

"Call us anything you want.
Call us **makeshift champions**.
We don't care."

Bobby Knight (*Up Close Primetime, 1996*):

"The will to prepare to win is so much more important than the will to win. When they're throwing it up, everybody wants to win, but how much has everybody wanted to win on Wednesday, Thursday and Friday getting ready for Saturday's game?"

Brett Favre (*Up Close Primetime, 1997*):

"We're out there on that field for one thing. It's not for the glory, it's not for the money, it's not for all the fans to love you. It's to win."

Rick Pitino, on coaching at the University of Kentucky (*Up Close Primetime, 1996*):

"You entice a coach here with winning. You're at the Roman Empire of college basketball."

U.S. national soccer team forward **Eric Wynalda**, on beating
Argentina 3-0 in the COPA America (*ESPN.SportsZone, 1997*):

"It was 10 years of hard work put into one game.
The cool thing was that we made Diego Maradona cry. When asked
why he was crying, he said it wasn't because Argentina lost,
but that America was playing such brilliant soccer."

Shaquille O'Neal (*Up Close Primetime, 1997*):

"Winning **the NBA title** is very, very
important to me. **I've won on every level
except college.** I haven't won in college
because, you know, **I left early.**"

Steve Spurrier (*Up Close Primetime, 1996*):

"Byron Nelson said, 'You can't take money
to your grave, but you can take titles and
championships.' So when my coaching
days are over, they're not going to say how much
money he made as a coach, they're going to say,
How many championships did he
win? And hopefully it's a bunch of them."

John Elway (*Up Close, 1997*):

"If I never get a Super Bowl ring, at least I can wake up in the morning, get up, brush my teeth, look myself in the mirror and say that I did everything I possibly could do to get it done and it just didn't happen."

Chris Berman, after the Broncos defeated the Packers 31-24
to win Super Bowl XXXII (*SportsCenter, 1998*):

"This **cements** John Elway's **place in history**. By the way, it's a place that's **been there for him all along**."

John Elway, at the Broncos Victory Rally (*ESPNEWS, 1998*):

"Isn't it **fun** to stick that **one** finger in the air and say, **'We are the best!'**"

Bobby Bowden (*Sunday Conversation, 1991*):

"There's about a foot difference between a halo and a noose."

The Agony of Defeat

Charles Barkley (*Up Close, 1994*):

"I hate losing more than I like winning."

Jim Kelly (*Up Close, 1997*):

"If someone's judging my career on going to four Super Bowls and falling short, they've never been a fan of football and they have no idea what they are talking about."

Sam Wyche (*"Winning and Losing," Outside the Lines, 1993*):

"A few years ago I was rubbing genius dust off my shoulder, and suddenly I've become the biggest blooming idiot in the league. That's part of the scoreboard mentality."

One-time national champion **Bobby Bowden** (*"Winning and Losing," Outside the Lines, 1993*):

"After six years, I finally found out what the big one is – it's the one you lose."

Troy Aikman, after the Cowboys' disappointing 1996 season
(*Sunday Conversation, 1997*):

"I'm **not as proud** as I **once was**."

Lou Holtz (*Up Close, 1997*):

"If I finish **second** in the country at Notre Dame,
everybody calls me an **idiot**. If a guy finishes last in
medical school, they all call him **doctor**."

Tony Kornheiser, on Greg Norman's collapse in the final round
of the 1996 Masters (*The Sports Reporters, 1997*):

"Norman must have died a thousand
deaths out there. People who wanted him
humbled got more than they asked for. Who
knows if Norman will ever win another major,
but I think I'm on the side of the angels
when I say I'm rooting for him."

Greg Norman (*Sunday Conversation, 1997*):

"I screwed up."

Bill Murray, on how the media treated Greg Norman after he blew his six-stroke lead (*Up Close, 1996*):

"When someone has a bad day like
that on the golf course, you say, Greg, you
look good, you look fantastic. I like
your shoes, I like your pants, I like your . . .
well, the hat's okay. I mean, you need to keep
it light. Instead they say, Greg, what's next?
Suicide? Alcoholism? Drugs?"

Pat Riley, after the Bulls eliminated the Heat in the Eastern Conference finals (*SportsCenter, 1997*):

"Sometimes you can **build a team** and have a great team that could be a **championship team**, and you **never win a championship** because you had the **misfortune** of being born at the same time that **Jordan went through his run**."

Michael Jordan's response (*SportsCenter, 1997*):

"It gives me **great pleasure** to make sure **he's denied**."

Bruce Coslet, on what was wrong with the 1997 Bengals (*NFL Countdown, 1997*):

{ "We can't run. We can't pass. We can't stop the run. We can't stop the pass. We can't kick. Other than that, we're just not a very good football team right now." }

Richard Nixon, on how he responds to the losers in a championship ("*All the Presidents' Games,*" *Outside the Lines, 1992*):

"**I always write the losers**, because I know that **when you win** you hear from **everybody**, but when you lose, **you hear from your friends**."

Chris Webber, on how he felt after calling the time-out that may have cost Michigan the 1993 NCAA Championship (*Up Close, 1993*):

"I worked this hard, shooting every day, **sacrificed**, didn't go on vacations, playing **this sport I love**. God, why me? Why is this **happening to me?**"

Chris Webber (*Talk 2, 1994*):

"I'm **more** than **20 seconds** of a **man** or a **basketball player.**"

Falcon **Terence Mathis**, on the team's 0-7 start in 1996 (*SportsCenter, 1996*):

"If you don't **produce** on Sunday, there's **no fame**, there's **no money**, there's **no cars, no jewelry, no home**. And there's **no women**, because **who wants a loser?**"

Richard Nixon (*Up Close, 1992*):

"The fact that **you lose** doesn't mean **you're finished**. You're only finished **when you quit**."

Jim Leyland, on the Pirates' 1992 loss to the Braves in the National League Championship series (*"All the Presidents' Games," Outside the Lines, 1992*):

"It was almost like looking at a **Little League game**: one side **jumping up and down** and one side **bawling**."

Bill Laimbeer, on what he did after the Pistons lost to the Lakers in the 1988 NBA Finals (*Sunday Conversation, 1993*):

"We took some bottles of champagne from the Lakers locker room and came back and I sat down on the floor of the shower with the shower running over me, drinking my champagne and crying."

Rick Pitino (*Up Close, 1997*):

"Losing is not easy, but **you have to lose in order to win**. You don't like losing, no one does, but **the journey is the best part** of the trip."

Utah Coach **Rick Majerus,** on his team's chances versus Rick Pitino's Wildcats in the NCAA Tournament (*March Madness Finals, 1996*):

"I'd have a **better shot** at **Rogaine taking hold** than us beating Kentucky."

Rick Majerus, after Utah lost 101-70 to Kentucky (*SportsCenter, 1996*):

"I think I'm going to have about **10 of those Fuzzy Navels** and just call it a night."

CHAPTER 3

[*I'm the man*]

So we're shooting one of those *This is SportsCenter* promos and the bit has Stuart Scott and me trying to get seemingly reluctant Laker Kobe Bryant and Jet Keyshawn Johnson to stand up and be noticed. We take turns admonishing the rookies for their timid delivery of "I'm the Man." The rookies put on a good act, especially Keyshawn. During a break, in a great display of honesty, he says, "This is funny — you guys trying to get me to say, I'm the Man. The thing is, I *am* the Man." Keyshawn was funny. Keyshawn was wrong. Jerry Rice is the man. And Jerry Rice doesn't say such things. –KENNY MAYNE

Wayne Gretzky, on if he still likes being called The Great One (*Up Close, 1996*):

"I'm more comfortable with people just calling me **Wayne**. There's been a **couple of stretches** in my career where I probably could have been **The Good One** or **The Mediocre One**."

Jerry Rice, on how he feels when people say he is the best wide receiver playing today (*Sunday Conversation, 1995*):

"You will **never** hear me **say that.**"

Walter Payton (*Talk 2, 1994*):

"I'm a 9-to-5 guy: I carry my lunch in a lunchpail, and it's a tin lunchpail, and when work is over I go back home."

Andre Agassi (*Sunday Conversation, 1995*):

"Sometimes I'll get recognized out somewhere and then the next question they ask me is what I do."

Jackie Joyner-Kersee (*Up Close, 1996*):

"All I ever wanted to do was
give a great performance.
If people label me the world's greatest female
track athlete, I appreciate it, I accept it, but
I keep it in perspective. I know
there is always going to be someone else."

Barry Sanders, on why he doesn't strut after scoring (*Sunday Conversation, 1994*):

"Usually it just doesn't come to mind. I'm tired, I want to get back to the bench."

Nick Bakay, on Deion Sanders (*Super Bowl Live, 1996*):

{ "Clearly on the seventh day the good Lord did not rest, but set about creating an ego so leviathanic it towers over the trembling game it dwarfs. Lo, behold yonder warrior: the speed merchant fueled by desire and that ephemeral voice that says, Just don't ask me to tackle anyone." }

Got Milk spokesperson **Steve Young**, on being kidded by teammates about his wholesome image (*Up Close, 1996*):

"I've matured into soda now."

49er linebacker, **Gary Plummer**, on Steve Young (*NFL Prime Monday, 1995*):

"He's not very worldly. He doesn't dress like *Gentleman's Quarterly*. I mean, nothing like it. His motto is, **If it's free, it's for me**."

Pete Sampras (*Sunday Conversation, 1995*):

> **"I do have a personality.** The people that know me know that."

Jimmy Roberts, on Tiger Woods's persona (*ESPN.SportsZone, 1997*):

"What is often mistaken for **aloofness** and **arrogance** is really nothing more than the demeanor of a **basically shy** and **reticent young man**. Just remember, when you were 20 years old, **how do you think you would have handled all of this**?"

Roger Clemens (*Up Close, 1991*):

"Everybody kind of perceives me as **being angry.** It's not anger, **it's motivation.**"

Larry Bird (*Sunday Conversation, 1991*):

"A lot of people tell me I'm black on the inside and white on the outside."

Michael Jordan (*"The Ego Game," Outside the Lines, 1993*):

"Ego is everything."

Bob Ryan, on Michael Jordan's statement that he'd retire if Phil Jackson left the Bulls (*The Sports Reporters, 1997*):

> ## "Who does **Michael Jordan** think he is? **Michael Jordan**?"

Larry Holmes (*Sunday Conversation, 1992*):

"I feel I'm the best thing ever to happen to this world. I think God blessed me. I'm the greatest thing ever. I love me! Thank God for Larry Holmes."

Keyshawn Johnson (*"The Transition Game," Outside the Lines, 1996*):

"**I'm not cocky** – I'm confident. You know, there's a difference."

Decathlete **Dan O'Brien** (*SportsCenter, 1996*):

{ "I think my destiny is to become the world's greatest athlete." }

Martina Hingis (*Up Close*, 1997):

"IT FLATTERS ME TO BE COMPARED TO TIGER WOODS, BUT I ALWAYS SAY, **I'M EVEN YOUNGER**. **I'VE HAD MORE SUCCESS** IN TENNIS. I'VE REACHED A LITTLE MORE."

Buddy Ryan, on Buddy Ryan (*SportsCenter*, 1995):

"Buddy Ryan knows a hell of a lot more about offense than most offensive coaches do."

Frank Deford (*"The Ego Game," Outside the Lines*, 1993):

"There are an awful lot of athletes who can get to the 17th hole but are going to find a way to bogey on the 18th hole. Ego is the one who's going to birdie the 18th hole."

Martina Navratilova (*"The Ego Game," Outside the Lines*, 1993):

"Give it **any** kind of connotation that you want, **ego means what you're all about.**"

Albert Belle (*Up Close*, *1997*):

"I may not smile all the time, but **I am happy out there** to be out on the field. Even though **I may go 0 for 4 with 4 strikeouts**, I'm still happy that I can go out on the ball field and still **fulfill a lifelong dream**."

George Foreman, on his mean former persona and his likeable new one (*Up Close Primetime*, *1997*):

"I say to people all the time, this George Foreman is spending that George Foreman's money."

Reggie Jackson (*Sunday Conversation*, *1993*):

"I won't be forgotten. It just won't happen."

Deion Sanders, on his persona off the field (*Sunday Conversation*, *1992*):

"You can't think about how I am on the field and expect me to take it home. Do you think **I cut around the furniture and high step?** I can't help it if I get excited about my job."

Bill Laimbeer (*Up Close, 1996*):

"I wouldn't call myself a whiner. I'd call myself an intelligent player who saw a lot on the basketball court that the referees sometimes didn't see in the proper way – so I would let them know."

Joe Theismann (*"The Ego Game," Outside the Lines,1993*):

"**Ego is armor**. People with the biggest egos, to a large degree, are probably the most **insecure** people you'll find. **I know I am**."

Bobby Knight (*Up Close Primetime, 1997*):

"**How would YOU like to be a guy coming to take out my daughter?**"

Tonya Harding (*SportsCenter, 1992*):

["You know, everybody makes mistakes.
I can't be perfect all the time."]

O. J. Simpson (*Up Close, 1989*):

"I read onoe that the purest form of conceit is to be humble. **I think I'm a humble guy**, so I guess I am **a little conceited**."

The Worm

Dennis Rodman, on his persona (*Up Close, 1997*):

"I'm a regular guy: I go home, I take a shower, I do this,
I do that. But once I go out **I like to be free and dress the
way I want** to dress and act the way I want to act. And after that,
Black Moses has got to take his cape off and go to bed."

William Rhoden (*The Sports Reporters, 1996*):

"Under David Stern, the **NBA's mantra** became
Image is Everything. Dennis Rodman has devised a
clever **parody** of Stern's mantra and taken it to a
new level. **Rodman is the NBA's mirror**, and what
bothers Stern, more than the hair, more than the eyeshadow,
is that when he looks at Rodman, he feels **in an odd
way that he is looking at himself**."

Bulls owner **Jerry Reinsdorf** (*Up Close, 1997*):

"If Dennis Rodman had no tattoos and no
earrings and his hair were black and he led the NBA in
rebounding for five consecutive years, he probably
wouldn't be making any money off the floor."

Bobby Knight (*Up Close Primetime*, 1997):

"Dennis Rodman makes Titanic Thompson, Bobby Riggs and Barnum and Bailey all look like amateurs. There is the greatest hustler that man has ever seen."

CHAPTER 4

There is no *I* in ESPN. Just like the athletes we cover, we here at the Worldwide Leader in Sports need teammates. Mine, more often than not, is Stuart Scott - and I don't have to tell you that there is no *I* in Stuart Scott, either. In fact, we're trying to get those anchors who do have an *I* in their names to use *y* instead, as in Chrys Berman, Dan Patryk, Chrys McKendry, Byll Pydto, Myke Tyryko. . . . It's worth that extra effort, because that's what being a teammate, sans *I*, is all about. —RYCH EYSEN

Pete Sampras, on his relationship with Andre Agassi (*Sunday Conversation, 1995*):

"We're not going out to dinner during Grand Slams, but we get along."

Ken Griffey Jr., on being a Mariner (*Sunday Conversation, 1995*):

"I was at home when Jim Leyritz got hit by Randy Johnson. I jumped in my car, drove all the way down, got dressed and ran down to the bullpen and watched the game from there. If something was going to happen, I wanted to be there."

Magic Johnson, on leading the late-'90s version of Showtime (*SportsCenter, 1996*):

"YOU'RE TRYING TO GET THE GUYS TO UNDERSTAND THIS IS HOW YOU DO IT, AND **THEY WERE FIGHTING ME**. THEN I BUMP INTO THE REFEREE AND NOW ALL OF THEM ARE SAYING, OKAY, **YOU'RE ONE OF US NOW**. NOW WE'LL LISTEN TO WHAT YOU HAVE TO SAY."

Michael Jordan, on his minor-league baseball teammates (*Sunday Conversation, 1995*):

"**They had an attitude** toward the game that they truly loved because it was just a game, **it was a dream that they were fulfilling.** I kind of lost that in the realm of what was happening to me two years ago with basketball. **I was on a pedestal for so long** that I forgot about the steps to get to that."

Kevin McHale, on Celtics fans' perceptions of him and Larry Bird (*Sunday Conversation, 1993*):

"**They assumed that two white kids from the Midwest automatically were roommates and apartment-mates.**"

David Aldridge, on the Mavericks' former tandem of Jimmy Jackson, Jamal Mashburn and Jason Kidd (*SportsCenter, 1997*):

"The only three Js that turned up in Dallas were jealousy, jawing and juggling lineups."

George Bush, on which other president he'd want as a teammate
(*"All the Presidents' Games," Outside the Lines, 1992*):

> "I'd take **Lincoln as a partner,** hoping that
> **he'd hit the long ball** because he was six feet four."

Scottie Pippen (*Sunday Conversation, 1994*):

"I am a player
without Michael."

Mike Lupica (*The Sports Reporters, 1995*):

"David Stern is another talented member of Michael Jordan's supporting cast. He'll get used to it. Scottie Pippen did."

Charles Barkley, on whether he'd kiss Michael Jordan before a game like Isiah Thomas did with Magic Johnson in 1988 (*Sunday Conversation, 1993*):

"I can see that it's **a good financial decision** to get in a relationship with him but **lookswise**, he's **not that handsome**."

Karl Malone, describing himself and John Stockton (*SportsCenter, 1997*):

"What you see is what you get. I always say, We're not the limo guys. We don't wear the double-breasted suits."

Darren Daulton, on then-Philly teammate John Kruk (*SportsCenter, 1991*):

"It's not over till the **fat man swings**."

Former Brave **David Justice,** on Greg Maddux (*Up Close Primetime, 1996*):

"The **one person that I hated in baseball** is born on the same day, same year as me, and is on my team."

Chipper Jones, on his reaction when David Justice and Marquis Grissom were traded by the Braves to the Indians (*Up Close, 1997*):

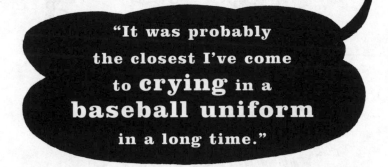

"It was probably the closest I've come to crying in a baseball uniform in a long time."

Former Oilers coach **Jerry Glanville,** on team discipline (*Sunday Conversation, 1991*):

"You're not allowed to fight on the first bus. If you want to fight someone on our team, you've both got to get on the second bus. So we have rules."

Joe Magrane, on former White Sox teammate Frank Thomas (*ESPN Major League Baseball, 1997*):

"He's so big, **he could drink a gallon of milk** and it would go sour before it got to his stomach."

66

Charles Barkley, on being traded to the Rockets (*Up Close Primetime, 1997*):

["Good help is hard to find. I just wish I had got traded to play with these guys sooner."]

Lou Holtz (*Up Close, 1997*):

"The **only friends** you have in this world when things don't go well are those you **eat with, sleep with, pray with and cry with** – and that involves your family and your teammates."

Mickey Mantle Jr., on his father's relationship with Billy Martin (*ESPN.SportsZone, 1996*):

"They were **very competitive** in things like golf and backgammon. Those were the only times **I ever heard them argue.**"

Dan Patrick, on Dennis Rodman being traded to the Bulls (*SportsCenter, 1995*):

"Dennis Rodman, Michael Jordan and Scottie Pippen on the same team. A trio made in basketball heaven? Or something like teaming Snoop Doggy Dogg with Bach and Beethoven?"

CHAPTER 5

Is John Cook a better golfer than Jack Nicklaus? Well, if you check the all-time PGA Tour earnings list, he's ahead of the Golden Bear. That ought to prove just how valid money is when it comes to measuring what an athlete's worth. On *SportsCenter*, we spend a lot of time reporting on $100-million-plus salaries. For $250, I can take my family to an NBA game, watch a player throw a towel in his coach's face, stay till the final buzzer and fight traffic all the way home. This numbing comparison only underscores that today's walking conglomerates still need to earn something more difficult than dollars. Respect. —JACK EDWARDS

"It ain't **how much you make**, it's how **much you've got left.**"

Larry Holmes (*Sunday Conversation, 1992*):

> "I got into this business because I got tired of **beating up people for free**."

Michael Jordan (*"The Sport of Money," Outside the Lines, 1992*):

> "**I play** the game because **I love** the game. I get paid because **it's a business**."

Wilt Chamberlain (*Up Close, 1997*):

> "The only guy who's worth the money he's making is Michael Jordan. And maybe he should get 10 percent of everyone's salary."

Bob Ley, on today's superstars (*"The Sport of Money," Outside the Lines, 1992*):

> "**Reality says** these athletes now play for the **leagues**, the **networks** and the **sponsors**. In truth, they play for **fun**. Not theirs, but **ours**."

Chris Berman, repeating Babe Ruth's response when told he made more money than then-president Herbert Hoover (*"All the Presidents' Games," Outside the Lines, 1992*):

> "Hell, I had a **better** year."

Frank Robinson, fourth on the all-time home run list (*Up Close Primetime, 1996*):

"What bothers me is a first-year guy, a guy that hasn't played one day in the big leagues, makes more than I made in 10 years."

Adidas vice-president **Sonny Vaccaro** (*"Days of Madness," Outside the Lines, 1993*):

{ "There are **no amateur athletics**. The NCAA and the Final Four, the whole thing, **it's a business deal.**" }

Rece Davis (*SportsCenter, 1996*):

"**Senior Day**, a **special** time at any school, a time to **pay tribute** to the guys who have given **four years** of **blood**, **sweat** and **tears** so the coach can get **a great sneaker contract**."

Jamal Mashburn, on leaving Kentucky before graduating (*"It's a Mad, Mad, Mad, Mad Game," Outside the Lines, 1995*):

"It's a **business** decision. If you **get hurt**, you made a **bad business decision.**"

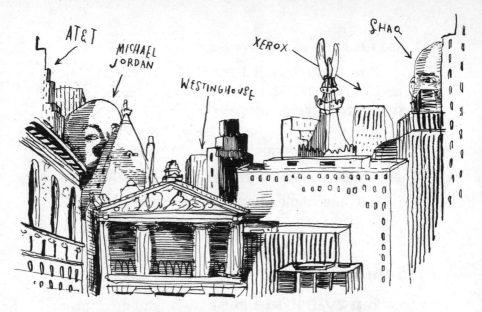

Chuck Daly (*"Coaching in the '90s," Outside the Lines, 1993*):

"If you **read the paper** and you follow the **Michael Jordans** or you follow the **Shaquille O'Neals**, these are all **multicorporations**, they are **not just people** running around in **short pants**."

Warrick Dunn, announcing he would stay at
Florida State for his senior year (*SportsCenter, 1996*):

"I haven't had money for 21 years.
What's another year?"

Jerry Stackhouse, on receiving endorsements before
playing in his first NBA game (*Up Close, 1997*):

"Basketball is a sport where people **get paid for their potential** more so than what they've accomplished."

Kevin Garnett, on how he'll deal with the pressure of his
$127-million contract (*Sunday Conversation, 1997*):

"I'm not God. I'm not Superman. You have some bad nights."

Charles Barkley, on NBA salaries in the late '90s compared to when
he entered the league in 1984 (*Up Close Primetime, 1997*):

"You guys didn't get a hundred million dollars because you were worth it. You got it because you were just born later."

John Feinstein, on the priorities of NBA rookies (*The Sports Reporters, 1996*):

"They don't look at Michael Jordan and say,
I want the rings. They look at Michael Jordan
and say, **I want my own shoe**. I want the
commercials. I want to be in movies like Shaq. It's not
about winning. **It's about endorsements**."

Shaquille O'Neal, announcing his seven-year, $120-million deal with the Lakers (*SportsCenter, 1996*):

{ "MONEY WAS **NOT THE MAIN FACTOR** HERE. I THINK PEOPLE GET TIRED OF HEARING **MONEY, MONEY, MONEY, MONEY, MONEY, MONEY**. I JUST WANT TO **GO AND HAVE FUN**, **BE YOUNG**, **DRINK PEPSI**, **WEAR REEBOK** AND **HAVE FUN**." }

Dick Schaap, on escalating NBA salaries (*The Sports Reporters, 1996*):

"The purpose of these new salaries is to teach the new math. When we were kids, we learned numbers from figuring out **batting averages** and things like that. But now you figure it out by trying to find out what the **average salary** is for a player over his career. Most of the players can't figure it out. Most of us can't figure it out."

Bill Murray, with the fan's perspective (*Up Close, 1996*):

"I had tickets to the Knicks, but they raised the price too much. It was bad for my image. I could afford it, but you could do the same thing by ripping up $20 bills in people's faces."

Andre Agassi, on being a millionaire athlete (*"Sports, Inc.," Outside the Lines, 1996*):

"Even though I'm on a salary, I still don't have a comprehension of what the real world functions like."

Felipe Alou, on why baseball needs to rethink its salary and revenue structure (*"Play Ball," Outside the Lines, 1995*):

"Otherwise, they are going to have to realign the major leagues and have a major league of the rich and a major league of the poor."

Lou Holtz (*Up Close, 1997*):

"There isn't anything wrong in this world with making money, as long as you make it honestly, spend it judiciously and are generous with it."

Don King (*Sunday Conversation, 1991*):

> "I'm not fighting a civil war, I'm fighting the poverty war. I'm looking for M-O-N-E-Y. I'm a capitalist."

White Sox vice-president of marketing **Rob Gallas**, on the difference between selling Bo Jackson and Michael Jordan (*"Jordan's Dream Spring," Outside the Lines, 1994*):

"We thought Bo was ELVIS. We were wrong. I mean, Bo was big, but MICHAEL is Elvis."

Monte Irvin, on racism and baseball salaries (*ESPN.SportsZone, 1997*):

"If you could play, **they'd pay you**. You'd get **equal salary**. Willie Mays was one of the **first guys** to make $100,000. When he made that, they gave **Mickey Mantle** $100,000."

Seahawk **Chad Brown** (*Up Close, 1997*):

"It becomes part of your name: Chad Brown, highest-paid linebacker. I'd much rather be Chad Brown, good father. Or Chad Brown, best friend. There's just so many other ways to describe me other than highest paid."

Peter Gammons (*SportsCenter, 1996*):

"After the **$8.1 million** earned by Hernandez and Fernandez in this country, maybe **Fidel Castro** should think about **balancing the Cuban budget** by **becoming an agent** for all the **Cuban players** who may **jump after the Olympics**."

Linda Cohn, on the debut of the New York Rangers' third jersey (*SportsCenter, 1997*):

"A **CAMEO APPEARANCE** FOR THE **STATUE OF LIBERTY** FOR THE RANGERS. **WHY** DO I THINK OF THE **FINAL SCENE** IN *PLANET OF THE APES*?"

Gary Player (*Up Close*, 1997):

"Too much **emphasis** is put on money, and **money** is **no criteria** to **judge a golfer. You've got to be a winner**, because there is a **big difference** between winning and **finishing second or third."**

Bob Stevens, on the John Daly-Tiger Woods pairing at the '97 Memorial Tournament (*SportsCenter*, 1997):

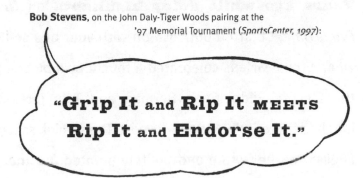

"Grip It and Rip It MEETS Rip It and Endorse It."

Dan O'Brien (*Up Close*, 1996):

"In '92, I'm wearing Reebok and I don't make the team, and in '96, I win the gold and I'm wearing Nike. So, what does that tell you?"

Frank Robinson, on escalating baseball salaries (*Up Close Primetime*, 1996):

"I think **Joe DiMaggio** described it best when they asked him **what he would be worth today.** He said, 'I'd walk in and say to the owner, **Hello partner.'"**

CHAPTER 6

Years ago while doing highlights on *NFL PrimeTime*, I blurted out, "Go on with your bad self!" when Ernest Givens celebrated a touchdown by doing the Electric Slide. Chris Berman and Tom Jackson laughed hysterically. Viewers loved it. Then a high school English teacher wrote and politely pointed out that I was setting a bad example by using a slang phrase every time a player did something strange. I wanted to reply, I'm just Robin having some fun with the boys, but that letter reinforced that we at ESPN are privileged to be role models as well as anchors. I never said, "Go on with your bad self!" again. –ROBIN ROBERTS

"Go on with your **bad self!**"

Anchor **Robin Roberts** (*SportsCenter, 1993*):

"Arthur Ashe is the **only athlete** who was a **role model** to me. I know we use that term loosely and a lot of young people say, So and so is my role model. I can **honestly** say that he is the only person, **only athlete**, I've ever looked to as a role model. He was someone who was **a mentor, a friend** – he was so many people. He was, by the way, **one of the greatest** tennis players of all time."

Arthur Ashe, on his announcement that he had AIDS (*SportsCenter, 1993*):

"The idea was not to try to get headlines, the idea was to try to make an impact."

Arthur Ashe, on taking a stance against Apartheid in the late '60s (*Portraits in Black & White," Outside the Lines, 1992*):

"You sometimes wonder, **why make all those sacrifices** if those coming behind you **don't want to step up to the plate** and be ready **to take a big swing.**"

Ken Griffey Jr. (*Sunday Conversation, 1993*):

> ## "I'm **not** a role model."

Rebecca Lobo (*Sportsmanship in the '90s Town Meeting, 1997*):

> "The athlete is not the one who decides whether or not they're a role model. It's the young kid out there who's watching you, and you respect that responsibility."

Charles Barkley, on why people shouldn't turn athletes into role models (*Sunday Conversation, 1992*):

> "The ability to run and dunk or hit 40 homers or rush for 1,000 yards doesn't make you God Almighty. And secondly, they shouldn't look up to somebody they can't be. They can't score and rebound like me. They can't run and jump like Michael Jordan. They can't pass the ball like Ervin Johnson. There's one or two guys out there – the other 99 percent have got to get a job, have got to get an education. They should be looking up to their parents."

Charles Sifford, on breaking the color line for other black golfers (*Up Close, 1989*):

"I didn't want anybody to give me anything. I just wanted a chance to play golf and prove to the world that a black man can play golf as well as a white man."

Hank Aaron (*Up Close, 1991*):

"I would like people **not to think in terms of the 755 home runs I hit** but think in terms of **what I've accomplished off the field** and some of **the things I stood for**."

Hakeem Olajuwon (*Up Close, 1994*):

"The way you play the game is how you are as a person."

George Foreman (*Up Close Primetime, 1997*):

"I had **two heroes**, John Wayne and Roy Rogers. Then one day **I saw Jim Brown** and I said, **That's the way I want to look**. Jim Brown represents **a dream come true for every young man** who wanted to be something, **especially in the '60s**. We saw in him **everything we wanted to be**."

Barry Bonds (*"Baseball, An American Portrait," Outside the Lines, 1994*):

"If you're just a normal person and you save a kid's life from actually getting hit by a car, that's a hero to me."

Billie Jean King, on Martina Navratilova coming out of the closet (*Up Close, 1993*):

"If any time you're causing someone to have to hide or lie, you're making a mistake. Our actions, our words, are supposed to match. Because Martina was truthful, because I was truthful – I didn't go out and murder somebody, I wasn't on drugs – we got penalized because of sexual orientation. It's pretty scary when you really analyze it because it's real important not to judge others, to blame others, but to accept responsibility for your own life. That's why we should praise people like Martina Navratilova, people who are true to their word."

Tony Meola, on being part of the launch of the MLS (*Sunday Conversation, 1994*):

{ "Maybe **20 years** from now I'll be watching *SportsCenter* and some young stud will say, **Thanks** to the **guys** in 1994 that **laid the groundwork** down for this league, we were **able to do** what we're doing today." }

Jimmy Johnson (*Up Close, 1996*):

"**I loved Hannibal Lecter**. Anybody that can talk somebody into killing himself by swallowing his tongue had to be **a pretty powerful speaker**."

Justin Leonard (*"The Tiger Woods Effect," Outside the Lines, 1997*):

"All of us need to write a thank-you note to Tiger for turning pro the way he did."

Dan Patrick, on Peyton Manning's decision to remain at the
University of Tennessee for his senior season (*SportsCenter, 1997*):

"Just when the media thought it had a **firm grasp** on the **stereotypical athlete**, along comes **Peyton Manning** to alter the mode."

Deion Sanders, after being criticized by Spike Lee for his flashy persona (*Up Close, 1991*):

"Well, I don't know if Spike Lee grew up in my community, where we had all the **drug dealers** with all the **gold chains** and all the **big, fancy cars**, and the children in my community looked up to all those guys. So **why can't I do the same thing**, without the drugs, **in a positive atmosphere**, and show the kids there's another way out – with education and school and sports?"

Kareem Abdul-Jabbar, on John Wooden (*Up Close, 1993*).

"I have tried to follow in his footsteps and be AS SUCCESSFUL a human being as he has been. The BASKETBALL IS A GIVEN, but the stuff that surrounds it, that's A LOT MORE IMPORTANT, and I see that now. Coach Wooden would not have had his success if he didn't have his own MORAL and ETHICAL BACKGROUND and his own INTEGRITY."

ABL guard **Jennifer Rizzotti** (*ESPN.SportsZone, 1997*):

"Someone needs to be **a positive role model** and **set an example** for young boys and girls to teach them that **sports isn't just about money.** Women play sports for the spirit of competition and the love of the game. That's **the only way** sports should be played."

Dennis Green (*Sunday Conversation, 1992*):

"I'm a product of the '60s, I'm a product of **Martin Luther King** and the **hopes and aspirations** of a guy being able to work his way up where everybody is judged on the content of his character and on his capabilities and **not on his race** and **religion** or on his **sexual preferences** or any damn thing else."

Magic Johnson (*Sunday Conversation, 1991*):

"I care about kids. I don't mind being a role model and I want to go out and speak about it and do all the things that really we should do as role models. I know a lot of guys don't want to take up that responsibility, but they should."

Chris Webber (*Up Close, 1995*):

"The more it seems that **some people shun me**, the more **the kids** in my community **gravitate towards me**, and **that's who I play for** – the young kids where I come from, in either New York or Michigan."

Walter Payton (*Sunday Conversation, 1991*):

"The role model starts at home. It's Dad and it's Mom, and if Dad and Mom aren't there, you look for outside people. If there is something in my life that I have done in the way I carry myself that can help other people, go for it. It's there, it's an open book, I don't have a patent on it. But you have to realize that I'm only human."

John Thompson (*Sunday Conversation, 1991*):

"We have led young people to believe everyone else is responsible for them. They'll say, I want you to make certain that little Johnny gets his schoolwork done. Well, hell, you look at the transcript, and he didn't do his schoolwork with them. So how in the world am I going to all of a sudden be a miracle worker and change them?"

Billie Jean King (*Up Close, 1988*):

"Because of the time I was born in history, being in the forefront of tennis and women's sports in the late '60s, early '70s, I created a lot of exposure. People got to see women athletes through the Virginia Slims circuit. What really helped, though, more than anything, would be the match with Bobby Riggs in 1973. I think psychologically people accepted the women as athletes and it said, Yes, we really do need Title IX. It kept reinforcing us going forward and being accepted."

Former Cowboys quarterback **Danny White**, advising young quarterbacks (*ESPN.SportsZone, 1996*):

"You have to have great discipline off the field. You have to be a great community citizen – basically, you have to live your life the way you would expect your heroes to live theirs. It doesn't hurt to have a great arm and a great mind, but it all starts in the classroom and the home."

"I am the only black woman sportscaster on the network level so **I know the pressures of being a role model** for young people. **Children of all colors idolize athletes** who perform superhuman feats. In the black community, especially, **we are constantly in search of people to look up to** and admire. Mike Tyson is someone I never want a child of mine to look up to. Out of the ring, **Mike Tyson constantly failed all of us.** Even in his testimony he dishonored us. Mike Tyson is **a tragic, misguided figure who has attracted too much attention** for his misconduct. No one relishes seeing a world-class athlete **cut down in his prime by himself.** Of course, I'll miss seeing him in the ring, but **I'm relieved that he has been found guilty.** This verdict is a relief to all women, but especially for **one quiet, humble, 18-year-old who stood up to Mike Tyson** the way no one else has, and today **this young woman is my hero.**"

"Behind every **kid's success** is an adult, and behind every **kid's failure** there is an adult. **We must help our kids** so they may **become our taxpayers** instead of our tax burdens."

Jim Brown (*Up Close Primetime, 1995*):

"Magic Johnson's a great role model because his work habits in basketball are impeccable. So is Larry Bird. They learned something new each year, they worked their butts off and then came back. I would say to my daughter, follow those work ethics if you want to play basketball."

Tony Gwynn (*Up Close Primetime, 1996*):

"When you sign that major league contract, there's some other things that are included that aren't on paper. You have to conduct yourself in a manner in which **you're going to be responsible.** And when somebody doesn't, you're just automatically **thrown in with them** because you're in the **same sport** or you're the **same skin color** or you make about the **same amount of money.**"

Emmitt Smith (*Up Close, 1996*):

"Each and every person on this planet is a role model. If we all just live the way man was intended to live, we don't have to worry about designating anyone as a role model."

One of Our Own

↓

Dan Patrick, on Tom Mees (*SportsWeekly, 1996*):

"He **never** wanted to **be bigger than the game**, never wanted to **be bigger than the story**. He just said, '**It's only sports**. Do it that way.'"

Bob Ley, paying tribute after Tom Mees' untimely death (*SportsCenter, 1996*):

"The night the Penguins won their first Stanley Cup, Tom was to interview Mario Lemieux. The live shot was still two minutes off, and everyone around Lemieux wanted him to leave and join the celebration. Tom asked, 'Mario, could you wait another minute for us?' Lemieux responded, 'For you, Tom, anything.' Tom would never tell that story. We heard it only after he died, from his producer."

CHAPTER 7

Since cash is king, look no further than The Suits to find the real kings of sports. They make the hires and sign the checks, therefore they make all the rules. (It's one of the few similarities between the sports world and the real one.) We have hands-on coaches with deceptive nicknames (The Tuna) and hands-on owners with dead right ones (The Boss). And then there's Jerry Jones, who doesn't need a nickname because he's got his hands on every title in sight as the Dallas Cowboys owner, general manager and assistant coach. – STEVE LEVY

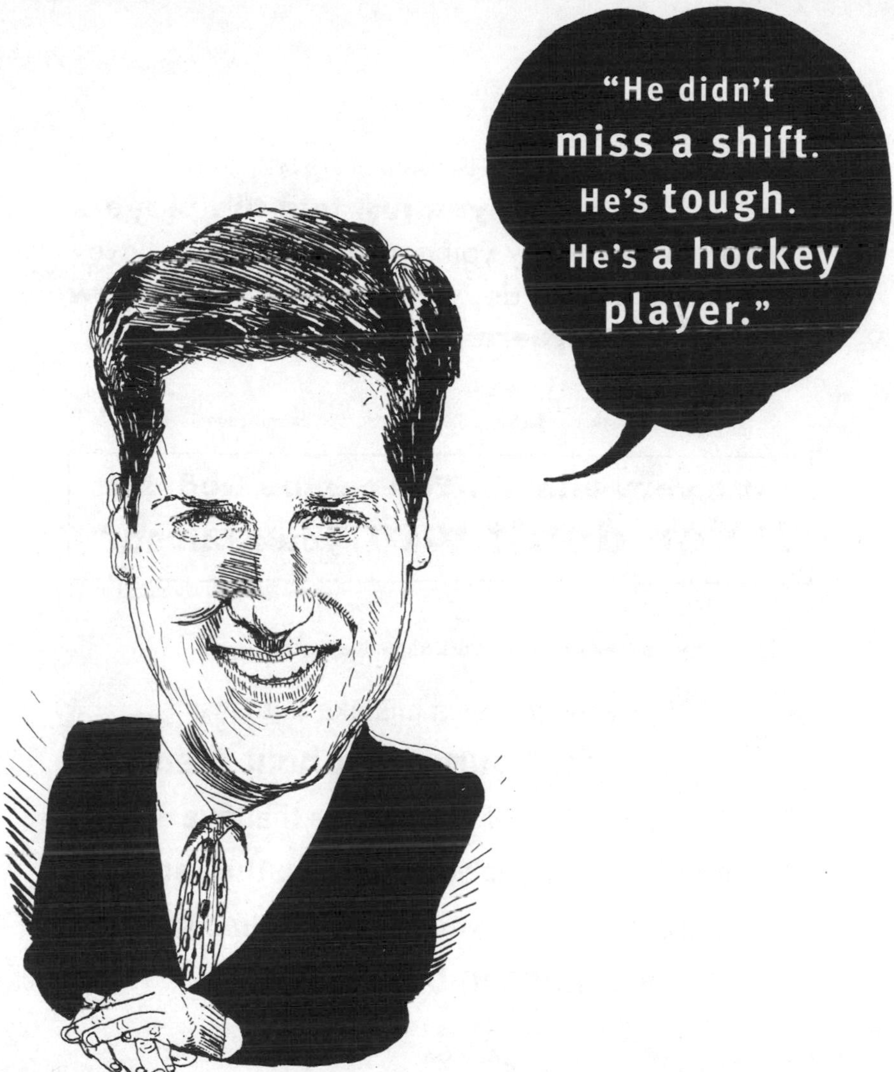
"He didn't miss a shift. He's tough. He's a hockey player."

Rick Pitino (*"Coaching in the '90s," Outside the Lines, 1993*):

"Back in the old days, **you just told the players what to do**. Today you can't do that — you have to tell them **what** to do, **why** they're doing it, **how** to do it and **where** it's going to lead them."

Beano Cook, on coaching college football (*SportsCenter, 1996*):

"It's very simple. You can be God, but **if you don't win,** you're fired."

Former Yankees manager **Buck Showalter** (*Up Close, 1997*):

"Everyone makes a mistake thinking something **can't survive without them.** Billy Martin told me one time that **five minutes after you've moved on, they are going to wonder who the next dumb guy is** coming in behind you."

Larry Brown, announcing his resignation from the Pacers (*SportsCenter, 1997*):

"Sometimes being a coach is like being a second lieutenant in a combat zone. Eventually you are going to get shot."

Anchor **Robin Roberts** (*"Coaching in the '90s," Outside the Lines, 1993*):

"Coaching in the '90s means coaching in a world in which the greatest athletes are often recruited by the streets."

Chuck Daly (*"Coaching in the '90s," Outside the Lines, 1993*):

"You've got to be a **con artist**, you've got to be a **disciplinarian**, you've got to wear **so many hats** I just don't know where it's all going to come from."

Pat Riley (*"Coaching in the '90s," Outside the Lines, 1993*):

"Coaching is an interactive relationship whereby it's my job to **elicit a response** in order to get a result, which is **to win**."

Bob Ley, paraphrasing Eugene McCarthy (*"All the Presidents' Games," Outside the Lines, 1992*):

"Being in politics is like being a football coach. You have to be smart enough to understand the game and dumb enough to think it's important."

Mitch Albom, on why Lou Holtz shouldn't consider leaving Notre Dame for the NFL (*NFL PrimeTime, 1996*):

"The players are more famous than you, they make more money than you, and when you urge them to win for the glory of their institution, they look at you as if you belong in an institution."

Earle Bruce (*"Coaching in the '90s," Outside the Lines, 1993*):

"A coach has got to be vocal and he's got to be tough in football. You're not playing a namby-pamby game of croquet, you're playing a game where someone's going to jam that helmet down your throat if they can."

Utah's **Rick Majerus**, on the difference between coaching in college and the NBA (*Up Close, 1997*):

> "The pro game **is like a stepparent:** you have the responsibility without the authority."

Jerry Glanville, on how you'd coach if you wanted people to like you (*Sunday Conversation, 1991*):

"You go in a corner, you get a glass of milk, you suck on your thumb and you let somebody else make the decisions."

Nick Bakay, on coaching basketball at UNLV (*Talk 2, 1995*):

"This has become one of the weirder gigs, the Bermuda Triangle of coaching. Tark and Rollie get ejected, Tim Grgurich snaps under the weight. You have to wonder if the Thomas & Mack Center was built on an old Indian burial ground, or is the ghost of the Rat Pack venting their anger that Vegas has gone family? Is Wayne Newton the only man for the job?"

Bill Murray, on if he ever wanted to be a baseball manager (*Sunday Conversation, 1993*):

"NO, THE PLAYERS THINK THE MANAGER **IS JUST A GEEK**."

Bill Parcells, on why he left the Patriots
for the Jets (*SportsCenter, 1997*):

"They want you to **cook the dinner**,
at least they ought to **let you shop**
for **some** of the groceries."

Jets owner **Leon Hess**, on hiring Bill Parcells as head coach
and chief of football operations (*SportsCenter, 1997*):

"I just want to be **the little boy who goes
along with him** and pushes the cart in the
supermarket and **lets him fill it up**."

Keyshawn Johnson, on his new coach, Bill Parcells (*Up Close, 1997*):

"I know he's been to **three
Super Bowls** and that's
enough for me."

Bill Parcells, on leaders he admires (*Up Close Primetime, 1997*):

"I like **Churchill, Truman—**
the **stand-up guys**, the guys
that **could hold the fort**, so
to speak, **under duress**."

98

Tom Landry, on his successor as coach of the Cowboys (*Up Close, 1996*):

"Jimmy Johnson, he can't stay too long. He's a motivator, and you can only motivate a team for so long. When that's over, you better move on."

Wayne Huizenga, announcing the hiring of Jimmy Johnson to replace Don Shula as coach of the Dolphins (*SportsCenter, 1996*):

"I'm here to announce today that we do not have any tickets available for the Dolphins/Cowboys game coming up this year."

Chris Myers, on Jimmy Johnson's history of following legends (*Up Close, 1996*):

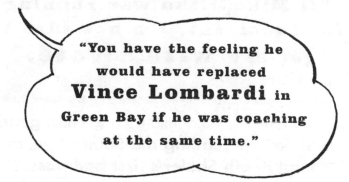

"You have the feeling he would have replaced **Vince Lombardi** in Green Bay if he was coaching at the same time."

Mike Ditka, on his outbursts (*Sunday Conversation, 1991*):

{ "Sometimes **our mouths** and reactions operate **before our brains get synchronized**, and that happens to me a lot." }

Mike Ditka, on why a player is like a diamond (*"Coaching in the '90s," Outside the Lines, 1993*):

"In its **native** state it's **nothing,** but in its final, polished state it's beautiful. How do you refine it and get it to the final stage? **You put it under heat, fire, pressure."**

President **Bill Clinton** (*"All the Presidents' Games," Outside the Lines, 1992*):

"If Mike Ditka was running for President, I'm not sure I'd get **my wife's vote.**"

Larry Beil, on Mike Ditka's comeback with the Saints (*ESPN Radio Network, 1997*):

"In New Orleans, we're told it's **a kinder, gentler Mike Ditka** now **leading the Saints**. Sure, at least **until Heath Shuler's first bad pass.**"

Rick Pitino, on rumors he would leave the University of Kentucky for the NBA (*Up Close, 1997*):

"I am not about to say that I'm going to break Adolph Rupp's coaching tenure here as far as longevity is concerned. I'm smart enough to live in the precious present. I don't mean to knock any other jobs, because they are all great, too, but I have the greatest job in all of basketball."

Mike Lupica, on the rumors surrounding Rick Pitino moving to the NBA (*The Sports Reporters, 1996*):

"TRYING TO DIFFERENTIATE BETWEEN WHAT RICK SAYS AND WHAT HE REALLY MEANS IS LIKE TRYING TO FOLLOW THE NEW *MISSION IMPOSSIBLE* MOVIE. HE THINKS ABOUT MAKING A MOVE AND HE STARTS TALKING ABOUT HIS KIDS AND HE STARTS SOUNDING LIKE JERRY LEWIS."

Larry Bird, on what he said to Rick Pitino when the Kentucky coach was interviewing with the Celtics (*Sunday Conversation, 1997*):

"If you come here, I'm going to get out of here, because I don't feel that you should come in and have to worry about me looking over your shoulder."

Bill Walsh, on his role as administrative assistant with the 49ers (*SportsCenter, 1996*):

"When I took the position, it was agreed from my side that I would have no power and no responsibility. Because either I have none, or I have it all."

Bill Walsh, on his not-so-well-defined role with the 49ers (*SportsCenter, 1996*):

"I don't like that **administrative assistant title**. It never has stuck well. That connotes **getting pizza orders** and **bringing in a fresh cup of coffee** for the coaches."

Jerry Rice, on Bill Walsh (*Up Close, 1996*):

"The **BEST coach** to ever coach the game."

Frank Deford, on Tony Dungy (*ESPN Radio Network, 1997*):

"He was stereotyped – not once, but twice. First, he was black. But second, he didn't fit the simple image of a pioneering black coach. That was supposed to be somebody obvious and outspoken, like Bull Russell, Frank Robinson, Art Shell. Dungy's leadership is subtle. He is a cerebral man who will patiently explain to an innocent like me how a defense works."

Jim Kelly (*Sunday Conversation, 1997*):

"Ask anybody who has been a Buffalo Bill player and has left this organization. Ask them who they miss the most, I'm sure they'll say Marv Levy."

Expos catcher **Darrin Fletcher,** on manager Felipe Alou (*SportsCenter, 1996*):

"He is kind of like that **biblical character** that's out in the mountain and you walk up 20 stories of rock and ice and stuff to get to the top and **there is Felipe on top** with a staff in his arm and he's preaching to you and telling you **the meaning of life.**"

Chris Webber, on his problems with then-Warriors coach Don Nelson (*Sunday Conversation, 1995*):

"This guy was on such a high pedestal, it was like, Oh my God, you dissed the god of coaching. It must be your fault."

Brett Hull, before Mike Keenan became head coach of the Blues (*Sunday Conversation, 1995*):

"Mike is a **very classy individual.** He's got a lot of charisma. He's the type of guy that I really like, so **I'm looking forward to it**. As long as personalities don't disrupt the team goal, **everything's going to be just fine**."

Bill Walton, on playing for John Wooden at UCLA (*Up Close, 1994*):

"**Two** hours of nonstop basketball, at the **highest level,** with the **greatest players** and with **the master** sitting there, critiquing everything, **never letting a single error go unnoticed** or uncriticized, yet **always pointing out the positive** things and building the team for the **championship** moment."

Jim Harrick, who coached the Bruins from 1988 to 1996 before being forced to resign for lying about having extra players attend a recruiting dinner (*Sunday Conversation, 1995*):

"I'm **stubborn enough** to want to be **the guy that lasted after John Wooden**."

Nebraska quarterback **Scott Frost**, on playing
for Tom Osborne (*SportsCenter, 1997*):

"WE DON'T **JUST PLAY FOOTBALL** AROUND
HERE. WE LEARN HOW TO BECOME GROWN-UPS,
HOW TO MATURE, **HOW TO BECOME MEN**."

Joe Morgan, on Sparky Anderson's main asset
("*The Big Red Machine*," *Outside the Lines, 1996*):

"He was able to get **25 guys**
pointed in the same direction,
and that direction was **winning**."

Jerry Glanville (*Sunday Conversation, 1991*):

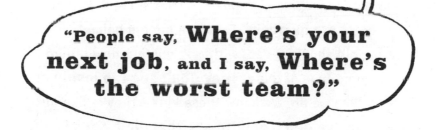

"People say, **Where's your**
next job, and I say, **Where's**
the worst team?"

Barry Melrose, on whether he'd consider coaching again (*ESPN.SportsZone, 1996*):
"I would love to **coach again**, but unfortunately, **GMs**
don't always like to hire people like me. They like
to hire **quiet people who do what they're told**."

Lenny Wilkens, on coaching Shaquille O'Neal at the NBA All-Star Game (*Up Close, 1994*):

"I was talking to Shaq about how to execute a drop step. He looked at me and said, 'Coach, have you ever played at this level?' The next day he wants to take a picture of me and him because he said he talked to his father and his dad said, 'Yeah, he was pretty good.'"

Jayson Williams, on John Calipari becoming coach of the Nets (*SportsCenter, 1996*):

> "I didn't think **Jesus** could coach this team, but I think **John Calipari** can."

Bobby Bowden (*Up Close Primetime, 1996*):

"To those thousands of alumni sitting up in the stands, **players are numbers**. They're a big old helmet, with a big old shoulder pad, with a 12 number down there. It's a hero type of thing. **They don't see the inside of them** like we do. We know these kids – they're like our children. **We don't want to see them fail**. So, a lot of times, we want to give them **a second chance**."

Dave Cowens, on being named coach of the Hornets (*SportsCenter, 1996*):

"I'm as ready as an **unmilked cow** at high noon. I'm drippin' ready."

Auburn coach **Terry Bowden,** on being compared to his father (*Up Close, 1994*):

"He's my mentor, but I don't think I can sit there and say I'm just like Bobby Bowden. I may be a lot like him **on the field** in my system of coaching and my style of leading, but personally **I think I'm more like my mother."**

Bobby Knight (*Up Close Primetime, 1996*):

"My wife was telling me about the **failure of positive reinforcement** in American education, that **everything Johnny does is okay**. You know . . . Johnny, I know you've missed seven shots in a row, but **don't let that bother you** – when you see the eighth one, just shoot it. I'd like to say, John, you know **you've missed two shots now, bad shots**. You take another one, **I'm going to strangle you**."

Joe Paterno (*Up Close, 1994*):

{ **"I tell guys, if I don't yell at you once in a while,** forget about it, **I'm not really interested in you. I've got to get inside** and make you **realize how good you can be."** }

Grant Hill (*Up Close Primetime, 1997*):

"People think of Coach Knight as some crazy wild man. But I've learned in my short career in basketball that every coach is a crazy and wild man. Especially the great ones."

Chris Berman, on Jerry Jones replacing Tom Landry with Jimmy Johnson (*SportsCenter, 1989*):

"You can't help but think of the coldness with which a legend was dealt. Money can buy a lot of things. Today it bought the Dallas Cowboys, but it doesn't buy class."

Jimmy Johnson, on Jerry Jones (*Sunday Conversation, 1994*):

"He's very egotistical. Just like I am."

Jerry Jones, responding to criticism about how he runs the Cowboys (*Up Close, 1996*):

"What you see is **a passion**. What you see is a way to figure out within the rules the best way to win. **I want to do it sensitively**, but I'm going to try and make the best decisions **no matter if it gets me kicked in the butt.**"

Sixers owner **Pat Croce**, on why he drafted Allen Iverson (*SportsCenter, 1996*):

"See these fingers? They're naked. He's my chance to get a ring."

Billy Martin as Felix

George Steinbrenner as Oscar

THE ODD COUPLE

Billy Martin, on George Steinbrenner (*Up Close, 1988*):

"George doesn't have a personality – he's The Boss. Personalities are for people who are working for the boss. Bosses do not have personalities, they have egos."

George Steinbrenner, on what made Joe Torre a great Yankees manager (*Up Close, 1996*):

"He's **a New Yorker**, native New Yorker. He's got **that mental toughness** that he needs and **he's a man's man**. He handles it."

Don Mattingly, on playing for the Yankees when George Steinbrenner was suspended from baseball in 1990 (*Sunday Conversation, 1993*):

"I really felt like I was **on a boat** in the middle of the ocean and there was **nothing but black** and it was **going nowhere**."

George Steinbrenner, on his All Star first baseman, Don Mattingly (*Up Close, 1996*):

"What Gehrig, Ruth, DiMaggio and Mantle were in their day, that is what Mattingly is to me."

ESPY host **Jeff Foxworthy**, after the Yankees lost Jim Leyritz, John Wetteland and Jimmy Key (*ESPY Awards, 1996*):

"George, congratulations on getting rid of all those **pesky World Series heroes**."

**"I have bled, I have cried,
and I have made this franchise
something that you'd be proud of.
We will build the GREATEST
shopping stadium facility
that the world has ever seen."**

"I just think it's great that the Braves didn't name their ballpark after some giant corporation but instead after a human being, a true American giant, an outrageous character with a Midas touch. A person who has promoted harmony throughout the world. A person who is as well known in Bulgaria as in Buckhead. I am speaking, of course, of Tina Turner, and while I personally would have preferred to have seen the field named after Henry Aaron, I am glad that the Braves, always politically correct, chose another distinguished African-American."

Retired Raider **Howie Long**, on Al Davis (*Sunday Conversation, 1994*):

"The **ironic** thing is that I've never seen him and **Darth Vader** in the **same place**."

Former Raider **Marcus Allen,** on his rift with Al Davis (*Talk 2, 1994*):

"I'm not afraid of him, because I stand by the truth. Some of these guys are under contract, some are gone and maybe they don't want to burn any bridges, but that's one bridge I wanted to burn."

Bulls and White Sox owner **Jerry Reinsdorf** (*Up Close, 1997*):

"I just **want to win**. I didn't get into sports **to make money**. There are a lot **better ways** to make money than **owning a sports team**. In fact, somebody once said that the best way to **make** a **small fortune** in **sports** is to **start out** with a **large** fortune."

Dick Schaap, offering advice to MLB owners (*The Sports Reporters, 1996*):

"Don't get mad at Jerry Reinsdorf. Get even. Approve the labor agreement with the Players Union. Raise the luxury tax and make sure it applies to all deals made after November 1, 1996. Reinsdorf has outwitted you all, which doesn't seem to be terribly difficult. He got you to reject the agreement, and then he sold you out. He signed Albert Belle to a $55-million contract. He raised the ante for all of you. Now you can call his bet, raise him back and, for a change, demonstrate a little talent and knowledge."

Tom Jackson, on Art Modell moving the Browns to Baltimore (*NFL Gameday, 1995*):

"I'm a **friend** of Art Modell. I say that first and foremost. But **what he has done has tainted every memory for every fan** who has ever supported that football team."

Mitch Albom (*The Sports Reporters, 1995*):

"Art Modell is **no hero** in this thing, but he didn't do anything that every sports icon hasn't done over recent years, which is **go for the money.**"

Nick Bakay (*SportsCenter, 1996*):

"**There will be no peace** on Lake Erie until the Dawg Pound gets to **toss Art Modell's head** around the stadium like a beach ball at a Foghat concert."

Art Modell, on what he would say to the over 200 chapters of the Cleveland Browns fan club (*Up Close Primetime, 1996*):

"Tell 'em to become members of the Ravens Roost. What do you want me to say? What do I say? I want to say thank you."

Bob Cousy, who had been mentioned in 1984 as
a potential NBA commissioner candidate (*Up Close, 1997*):

"Thank God they hired David Stern. David is
a bottom-liner with soul."

Dennis Rodman, on his relationship with David Stern (*Up Close, 1997*):

> "I'd like to take David Stern
> **as my prisoner, strip** off all
> his clothes, **rub lipstick and
> makeup all over him**, dress
> him up like Frank Sinatra and sing
> to him, 'I Did it My Way.'"

Charles Barkley, on David Stern and Dennis Rodman (*Sunday Conversation, 1996*):

"Thank God for Dennis. Dennis was a savior.
David Stern calls me now and says, You know what, I
apologize for all the things I said to you in the past.
Dennis is a lot worse than you are."

CHAPTER 8

Sometimes they beat on their chests and yell in their opponents' faces, "You can't hang with me." Sometimes they're like Michael Jordan, who said, "I don't need to yell – you'll know when it's over that I'm better." Pure, unadulterated competition. Somebody gives a great soundbite while champagne drips down her eyebrows. Somebody else can't give any kind of soundbite because he's lost his composure, sobbing in a towel. Not much has changed since Little League, except the champagne and the money. The beauty of this level of competition is that the champagne and the money don't mean a thing. –STUART SCOTT

"**Cool** as the other side of the pillow."

Martina Navratilova (*Sunday Conversation, 1993*):

"The other women are getting **embarrassed** when they lose to me because **I'm so damn old**."

Steve Young (*Up Close, 1997*):

"I'd rather be whipped physically than whipped mentally or emotionally. A quarterback would much rather get beat up and win then get booed and lose."

Cal Ripken Jr. (*SportsCenter, 1996*):

"If you were to ask me 14 years ago, can you play in 2,000 consecutive games, can you play in every single game for this amount of years, I'd say, no way, that's impossible."

Orel Hershiser (*Up Close Primetime, 1997*):

"In these days of attention deficit disorder, the playoffs are my Ritalin."

Bryan Cox (*Sportsmanship in the '90s Town Meeting, 1997*):

"When I'm out there **I try to cause pain. The three hours** I have to play **a game on Sunday** I can commit as many **crimes** as I want to **without going to jail.**"

George Foreman (*Up Close Primetime, 1997*):

"I had a meanness about me. I'd look at my opponent like **a man who's about to shoot a deer**: how is his head gonna fit on my wall as a trophy? To be **sized up** and **looked at as a prey** by a hunter is a frightening thing – to know that this man is not going to try to knock you down, **he's going to try to kill you.**"

Enos Slaughter (*ESPN.SportsZone, 1996*):

"The players now get a hangnail and they're gone for two weeks. I never heard of a hamstring or a rotator cuff until this generation."

Karl Malone, after Allen Iverson was named player of the week for recording his fifth consecutive 40-point game, all Sixers losses (*SportsCenter, 1997*):

"O and 5 and you score 40? So what? In this game, the name of the game is to **win with pride**, not **lose with pride**."

Martina Hingis (*Up Close, 1997*):

"So many players want to hunt me and beat me because I haven't lost for a very long time. I still think I have nothing to lose when I step on the court."

Walter Payton (*Up Close, 1994*):

["A lot of fans were **drawn to me** because they knew that whatever the score was, I was going to **run as hard as I could** on every play. You don't have that now, you have guys **waiting for next week** or **even next year**."]

Steve Spurrier, on Florida's reputation for running up the score (*Up Close Primetime, 1996*):

"How many points do you have to be ahead with, and how much time has to be left, when you're **not supposed to score again**? I can't get an answer on that. So we're not real smart around here. We just play the whole game, and when it's over we look up and see what the score is."

Detroit's **Aaron Ward**, on why the bad blood between the Red Wings and the Avalanche makes such great television (*SportsCenter, 1997*):

"It's **why you watch** the Discovery Channel – you like to watch **animals of prey take down predators, the alligators take out fish**. It's just **a natural human instinct** to want to watch."

Four-time gold medalist **Evelyn Ashford**, on how she would do against the top sprinters in the Atlanta Olympics (*Up Close, 1996*):

"At 30, I'd beat them. At 40, maybe not."

Larry Holmes (*Sunday Conversation, 1992*):

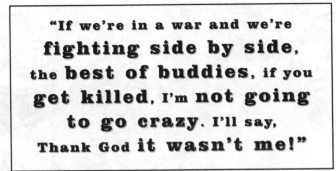

"If we're in a war and we're **fighting side by side**, the **best of buddies**, if you **get killed**, I'm **not going to go crazy**. I'll say, Thank God **it wasn't me!**"

Nick Bakay, on the rivalry between Florida and Florida State (*SportsCenter, 1996*):

"The Gators and the Seminoles **share a state, share a fever for football**, and yet **when they face off**, it's like someone spiked the water supply with something that **turns them** into **rabid hell hounds**."

George Brett, on the 1993 pine tar incident (*Sunday Conversation, 1992*):

"The next thing you know, they drop the bat down and measure it on home plate. As soon as they did that I said, 'You know, if they call me out, I'll kill them. I'll run out on the field and I'll kill them all right now.'"

Gail Devers (*Up Close*, 1996):

"I find my motivation within myself. I run track not from a competitive nature but because I'm a very goal-oriented person."

Reggie Miller, on his high-school rivalry with sister Cheryl (*Sunday Conversation*, 1994):

{ "I'm bragging, **'I had 39 tonight.'** And Cheryl was looking at me with this smile and **my dad's just giggling** and stuff, and she said, **'Well, I had 102.'"** }

NFL agent **Drew Rosenhaus**, on his competitive drive (*Up Close Primetime*, 1996):

"IS IT GOING TO TAKE **ME BEING THE PRESIDENT** TO BE **SATISFIED WITH MYSELF?** AM I GOING TO HAVE TO BE THE . . . **THE RULER OF THE WORLD**? I DON'T KNOW. AM I GOING TO HAVE TO **SET EVERY RECORD AS AN AGENT**? DOES EVERY ONE OF MY CLIENTS **HAVE TO BE THE HIGH-EST-PAID GUY** IN THE LEAGUE? DO I HAVE TO **REPRESENT EVERY PLAYER** IN THE NFL? DO I HAVE TO **OWN THE NFL**?"

Tom Glavine, on his justification for intentionally hitting a batter (*Sunday Conversation*, *1992*):

"If a **guy hits a home run** and he's going to point his finger at me, run around the bases and do cartwheels, **sure**. If he's going to **show me up**, **he's going to pay for it**."

Kenny Mayne, on NASCAR's Intimidator, Dale Earnhardt (*ESPN Radio Network*, *1997*):

"Imagine you're at the grocery store. You're told there's one T-bone left on special at $3.99. Only trouble? Dale Earnhardt scared the same info out of the assistant manager. You got your shopping cart out front, flying down past the canned vegetables, but Earnhardt's hungry, too. He may eat the steak raw. Now he's on your heels. In fact, he just ran over your left heel. Now you're side by side. He's staring you down. And suddenly, you feel like chicken."

Charles Barkley, on whether he loses his competitive edge playing against Michael Jordan (*Sunday Conversation*, *1993*):

["There's **nobody you'd rather beat** than your **good friend**."]

Shaquille O'Neal (*"Shaq's Sudden Impact," Outside the Lines, 1993*):

"I'm **not the type of guy** that'll say, oh, **my back was hurting,** I missed a free throw. **I was sick,** I missed a free throw. **I was just getting off the flu,** I missed a free throw. **If I miss 'em, I miss 'em."**

David Justice (*Up Close Primetime, 1996*):

"Would I go out in **stormy weather** across the street and **play baseball**? No. But **I might** go out in **freezing cold** in the snow and **play basketball."**

Grant Hill, on the frustrations of being an NBA lottery pick (*Up Close Primetime, 1997*):

"You're used to playing on **winning teams** in high school and college, being in the **state championship** or being in the **tournament**. And all of a sudden, you're **on a terrible team**, with guys **who have given up** and are thinking about the summer while **you're trying to prove yourself** and compete for rookie of the year honors."

Cardinals safety **Chuck Cecil** (*"Our Violent Games," Outside the lines, 1994*):

"You always need to look out for those guys who are willing to hurt themselves to hurt you."

Brett Hull (*Talk 2, 1994*):

"I've never had a **fight ever in my life**. There's nothing to get mad about. **Life's too short**."

Picabo Street (*ESPN.SportsZone, 1997*):

"I never doubted my ability, but there were times when I doubted my desire. And what, in fact, took my desire away had nothing to do with the sport. It had to do with everything around it."

Phil Jackson, on why he thought Scottie Pippen threw a chair after Toni Kukoc was given the last shot instead of him in a playoff game (*Sunday Conversation, 1994*):

"He thought he was the team, perhaps."

Kevin McHale (*Sunday Conversation, 1993*):

"I liked it better when everybody hated each other. Now everybody has the same agent and they hug and kiss after the game and you go, like, Man, this sucks."

Bob Ley, on Riddick Bowe joining the Marines (*SportsCenter, 1997*):

"Apparently **two consecutive fights** of Andrew Golota **punching Bowe's protective cup** were not **enough of a challenge**."

Riddick Bowe, on why he left the Marines after three days of boot camp (*Up Close, 1997*):

"I was **overwhelmed**, so I thought it **best** that **I just went home**."

Barry Sanders, on how defensive backs describe playing against him (*Sunday Conversation, 1994*):

"It's probably similar to **being in New York City** and **having a cab driver behind you** and you're driving too slow. **It's not the most pleasant thing**."

CHAPTER 9

Do you put a shwerve on? If so, how? And where precisely does one purchase a shwerve? Wal-Mart? Gucci? Foot Locker? While *SportsCenter* has a language, style and attitude uniquely its own, it also has a mandate to deliver all the news that fits into 60 minutes. All day, every day, responsibly, credibly, relentlessly. Over two decades, we've seen and reported it all: drafts and trades, playoffs and strikes. From bruised egos to bitten ears, spitting to Sprewell, Magic to Marge, natural wonders to natural disasters, America's team to America's most wanted. Now, has anybody seen my shwerve? —CHARLEY STEINER

"He's listed **day-to-day**, but then again, **aren't we all?**"

Charley Steiner, reporting on Tyson-Holyfield II (*SportsCenter, 1997*):

> "Evander Holyfield and a portion of his right ear arrived at Valley Hospital tonight. In separate cars."

Referee **Mills Lane**, on his conversation with Mike Tyson
after Round 2 in Tyson-Holyfield II (*Up Close, 1997*):

"When I went to his corner and said, 'That is going to cost you two points,' he said it was a punch. And I said, **'Bull____, you bit him**.'"

Roberto Alomar, on why he spit at umpire John Hirschbeck
(*"Major League Béisbol," Outside the Lines, 1997*):

"The **strong language** he used towards me, **he kind of offended me** as a person. It's a different meaning, it's a real strong meaning in **Puerto Rico**, and **I took it too personally**."

Bob Ley, on the suspensions of Patrick Ewing, Allan Houston,
Charlie Ward, Larry Johnson and John Starks following the Knicks-Heat brawl
in Game 5 of the Eastern Conference semifinals (*SportsCenter, 1997*):

"We've got the specter of **an entire NBA team** being called into the **principal's office**."

Chris Berman, putting the Broncos victory in
Super Bowl XXXII into perspective (*SportsCenter, 1998*):

"The image of the number 0 has been larger than life: 0-3 for Elway in the Super Bowl; 0-4 for Denver in the Super Bowl; 0-9 for the illustrious quarterback class of 1983; 0-13 for the AFC in Super Bowls since 1984. And, in one fell swoop, the 0-fers were goners."

David Aldridge, on Magic Johnson's re-retirement (*NBA Today, 1996*):

"It was clear and obvious that **Magic could not coexist** with Nick Van Exel, Cedric Ceballos, Eddie Jones. **They had to play one style,** he wanted to play another. He goes out now and **this frees up cap room** for the Lakers. Don't be surprised if they make a big push for **Shaquille O'Neal in free agency** this summer."

John Chaney, after college star Hank Gathers
collapsed and died during a game (*SportsCenter, 1990*)[1]

{ "Hank Gathers just epitomizes so much of what life's all about. The basketball meant nothing. The kid was a soldier for a lot of kids. He championed a lot of causes. To hear that he died just devastates me. How unfair is it?" }

Bob Ley, reporting from Candlestick Park during the strongest earthquake to hit San Francisco since 1906 (*SportsCenter, 1989*):

"I was in the upper deck. It was my first earthquake and for the first preliminary seconds I thought it was a fly-over perhaps of a low jet as part of the pre-game ceremonies. Within five seconds it became glaringly apparent that's not what it was."

Chris Berman (*Up Close, 1994*):

"My **two most memorable moments** at ESPN are both **in Candlestick Park**, which is fitting because I am an honorary Bay guy. **The Catch and the earthquake – the stadium moved** on both occasions."

Jimmy Roberts, on the impact of Tiger Woods's victory at the Masters (*SportsCenter, 1997*):

{ "It wasn't only about race, it wasn't only about youth, it wasn't only about power. The human tidal wave that crashed around Woods this week came in all colors, in all ages, sizes and strengths." }

U.S. Deputy Attorney General **Jamie Gorelick,** before the Atlanta Olympics (*SportsCenter, 1996*):

"Can we give a 100 percent assurance that there will be no mishaps, no events? No. No one could predict what will happen, but I think we're very well prepared – certainly as well prepared as we could possibly be."

Chris Myers, on the aftermath of the Olympic Park bombing (*SportsCenter, 1996*):

"Despite the improved security, the minute a loud noise is heard or a siren goes off, fans are going to fear danger more than they did before, and that will be the prevailing thought until these games are completed."

Bobby Knight, on the cocaine-related death of Celtics star Len Bias (*Up Close Primetime, 1996*):

"Lenny Bias **had the world in his hands** and stuck the world in a needle, stuck the needle in his arm, and **that's all there was to Lenny Bias.** Lenny Bias isn't sick, he isn't injured, he's dead, he's no more – and **it's a tragedy**, because here's a **kid that had everything**, everything in front of him."

133

Michael Irvin, during his trial for drug possession (*SportsCenter, 1996*):

> **"I'd rather be locked up as Michael Irvin than free pretending to be someone I'm not."**

Chris Mortensen, on the transformation of America's Team into America's Most Wanted (*SportsCenter, 1996*):

"I remember some Cowboy players lecturing the media about criticizing the way they traveled to practice in limousines. They said, We're Hollywood, we're like Hollywood stars. Well, what industry has more drug problems than Hollywood?"

Bob Ley, on the courtside stabbing of Monica Seles (*SportsCenter, 1993*):

"Fourteen years ago when we signed on, I don't think we really thought that what we would be reporting on a daily basis about sports would be so far removed so often from the final score."

Lenny Dykstra, the first major league player to speak out against the union's stance during the baseball strike (*Up Close, 1995*):

"Lenny Dykstra loves baseball. Lenny Dykstra's fortunate to be playing in the major leagues. Lenny Dykstra wants to be playing baseball again in 1995. As far as going across, you'll have to ask me again in April."

The Streak

Chris Berman, as Cal Ripken Jr. made his spontaneous lap around Camden Yards to celebrate starting in his 2,131st consecutive game (*Baseball Tonight, 1995*):

"If that **doesn't** make you **cry**, **excited**, **goosebumps** and all the above, then **check your pulse.**"

Cal Ripken Jr., on breaking Lou Gehrig's record (*SportsCenter, 1995*):

"I know that if Lou Gehrig is **looking down** on **tonight's activities, he isn't concerned** about someone playing one more consecutive game than he did. Instead, he's viewing tonight as **just another example** of what is **good** and **right** about **the American game.**"

Frank Deford, on female referees in the NBA (*ESPN Radio Network, 1997*):

"I'm all for opening up sports to more positions with women in authority. I want a woman to run the NCAA. That'll shake up all those mysogynist football coaches and athletic directors. And I want a woman to referee the next Mike Tyson fight. You spit that out immediately, Mike. I want a woman to run the Masters, so we'd get some style in those ugly green jackets. And, most of all, I want a woman to be commissioner of baseball. Of course, I'd settle just for a person to be commissioner of baseball."

The Choke

P.J. Carlesimo, at the start of the 1997 season (*Up Close, 1997*):

"In the NBA, **it's up to you to get along** and get this group to **be productive**. Because when you've got long-term contracts and **the amount of money that a player is making compared to what a coach is making,** you can't be **constantly** bringing situations to the GM or the President or the owner saying, Get rid of these guys. **How many guys can you get rid of**?"

P. J. Carlesimo, on the challenge of coaching franchise players
before Latrell Sprewell attacked him (*Up Close, 1997*):

**"You're certainly going to be a lot
better off** if you and your star players
are on the same page, so it's incumbent upon
you to get along. **But getting along
only goes so far:** that player needs to
respect you just as much as every
other player on the team, and that's a big
part of the challenge in the NBA."

Mitch Albom, on why the NBA was correct in banning Latrell Sprewell for
a year after attacking P.J. Carlesimo (*The Sports Reporters, 1997*):

"If David Stern didn't **take the action** that he
did, coaches would become **nothing more**
than **high-priced valets of players**."

Bill Conlin, on the respective futures of Latrell Sprewell
and P.J. Carlesimo (*The Sports Reporters, 1997*):

**"Latrell Sprewell will
play more games in the
NBA than P.J. Carlesimo
will coach."**

As Switzer's World Turned

Barry Switzer, after being named Jimmy Johnson's replacement
as head coach of the Cowboys (*SportsCenter, 1994*):

"We're going to run the same playbooks, the same defense. We've got the same coaches doing the same jobs. I hope I can do as good a job as Jimmy Johnson. That's what you're hoping, that's damn sure what Jerry's hoping, and that's why I'm here . . . I would be very upset if the team did not respond with fierce loyalty to the coach. That's what they should have . . . Nothing's going to change, Cowboys fans. Get ready to watch the Dallas Cowboys be the best in the NFL. We've got a job to do and we're going to do it, baby!"

Barry Switzer, announcing his resignation from the Cowboys
after four seasons, ranging from a Super Bowl victory in '95 to a
dismal 6 and 10 record in '97 (*SportsCenter, 1998*):

"I have a great loyalty with my coaches and everything and anything they do for me. I'm sad for them, but it's a happy day for me."

Barry Switzer, responding to reports Leon Lett would be found in violation of the NFL drug policy for the second time (*NFL PrimeTime, 1996*):

"I **don't** want to know. I **never** want to know."

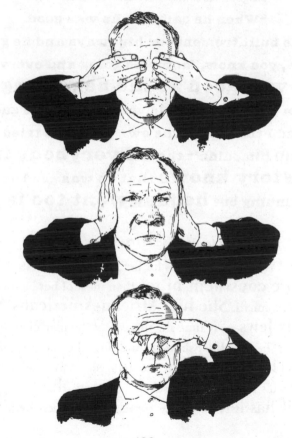

Marge Schott, on Adolf Hitler (*Sunday Conversation, 1996*):

"When he came in, he was good.
He built tremendous highways and he got
all the, you know, factories going and everything.
He was good at the beginning, but
then he went nuts. He went berserk, I guess,
and I think even his own generals tried to
kill him, didn't they? Everybody in
history knows that he was good at the
beginning but **he just went too far."**

Mike Lupica, on Marge Schott (*The Sports Reporters, 1996*):

"You have to say this for her, though. She is a
more consistent hitter than most of her ballplayers
in Cincinnati. She hits African-Americans. She
hits Jews every time she marvels at the marvelous early
speed she felt Hitler showed. And then she goes to another
field and hits Asian-Americans. She is as much a threat to
baseball's image and baseball's integrity, the integrity
it has left anyway, as someone like Albert Belle."

Marge Schott, apologizing for comments she had made
over the years regarding ethnicity (*SportsCenter, 1992*):

{ "I acknowledge in the past I have **on occasion made insensitive remarks** which I know hurt other people. On those occasions **it was my mouth but not my heart speaking**. For any such remarks which were **insensitive I am profoundly sorry** and apologize." }

Barry Larkin, on Marge Schott, who would be forced by the MLB owners
to leave baseball in 1996 (*Sunday Conversation, 1993*):

"I do feel that baseball is really the one thing that if it was taken away from Marge would crush her—other than her dog."

Marge Schott, when asked if she was happy (*Sunday Conversation, 1996*):

"Well, **I'm not ashamed**."

Magic Johnson, on how he contracted HIV (*SportsCenter, 1991*):

> "I did my best to **accommodate as many women** as I could, most of them through **unprotected sex.**"

Announcer **Mary Carillo,** on the impact of Magic Johnson's diagnosis (*SportsCenter, 1991*):

> "It was just **a loaded gun** waiting to go off. **All these jocks running around** the way they do and with all that's out there – I mean **I've always suspected** that it was going to happen at some point."

Boxer **Tommy Morrison,** after being diagnosed as HIV positive (*SportsCenter, 1996*):

> "I ask you to **no longer** see me as a role model, but see me as an individual who **had the** opportunity to be a role model and **blew it** with irresponsible, irrational decisions."

O.J. Simpson, on pleading no contest to assaulting Nicole Brown Simpson in 1989 (*Up Close*, *1989*):

"We had a fight, we were both guilty, no one was hurt, it was no big deal, and we got on with our life."

O.J. Simpson, on whether being a celebrity influences his behavior (*Up Close*, *1989*):

"I never wanted to be a victim of my celebrity, saying that I couldn't do that because I'm O.J. and the people don't expect it. What I do, I do if it's morally acceptable to myself."

O.J. Simpson, on why he thought he was charged with assault (*Up Close*, *1989*):

"The point was to bring attention to **a new law** that was on the books, and **who better to do that than me**? And I kept saying, **Why me?** Why am I the guy that you **choose to do this to?"**

"December 1973, I'm at the mall. I'm shopping for American history. There's a hero on TV. I'm mesmerized by the images on the rows of monitors at Sears. In the snow at Shea Stadium, O.J. Simpson goes past 2,000 yards, a junior high kid gets all emotional.

"A couple of decades later, the image gets real blurry. O.J.'s running real slow. Something about arthritis. Something about O.J. maybe eating a gun.

"Then the images get even freakier with the trial. Something about ice cream melting, dogs barking, DNA. Nothing in black and white. O.J.'s free. He gets his kids back. Fred Goldman doesn't get his.

"On to another lasting image. The President's on the air. Something about the races need to come together. The State of the Union nearly upstaged by the state of California. And a second jury takes O.J. down. And now the image is of O.J. driving home. He has his kids, something about stopping to buy ice cream."

Hindsight is 20/20, circa 1998

O.J. Simpson, after his acquittal in the criminal trial and conviction in the civil trial, on the one thing he would change about his life (*Up Close, 1998*):

{ "The **first thing** that **comes to mind** is that I don't think I would have **ever been unfaithful** to **either one** of **my wives**." }

O.J. Simpson, on whether he had ever hit Nicole Brown Simpson, who had kept a series of Polaroids documenting the 1989 assault (*Up Close, 1998*):

"No, I didn't. But I was very physical with her. You think if I hit you you'd be bruised? You'd be swollen, you'd be busted up a little bit . . . That's a picture with a Polaroid under a bad light at 3 o'clock in the morning. I'd like your wife to go take a picture and see what she looks like then. The point is, any bruise she had on her, I was responsible for. I have no excuses."

O.J. Simpson, on how he's coping with his situation (*Up Close, 1998*):

"When I read the Bible, from Moses to Jesus to Job, they all went through similiar things. That's what the Bible was for me – it was like a map that says things like this can happen in your life and you can overcome it."

145

O.J. Simpson, on whether he'd trade his life for Nicole
Brown Simpson's or Ron Goldman's (*Up Close, 1998*):

"I would have **put my life** certainly **on the line** for Nicole. **I loved her**. I honestly believe that **a kid needs a mother** more than they need **anyone**. The **most important person** in my life was **my mother**. . . But I would certainly be **lying** if I said I would trade with Ron Goldman. **I don't know Ron Goldman**. People die every day."

Pete Rose on Pete Rose

On what made him a great ballplayer (*Up Close, 1997*):

"God gave me **enthusiasm.** He gave me the **desire.** He gave me the **hustle.** God gave me the **determination.** I always **had to scramble** to get what I wanted."

On what he can still bring to baseball (*Up Close, 1997*):

"I think today I'm baseball's best ambassador. **Nobody** can sell the game the way I can."

On his greatest moment on the field (*Sunday Conversation, 1991*):

"I had **my Hall of Fame feeling** the night **I hit 4,192**. It took a **nine-minute standing ovation** for me to show that emotion. In nine minutes, you saw **three generations of Pete Roses** before you. You saw **me getting the hit**, you saw **me looking up to heaven** and **seeing my father**, you saw **my son Pete** coming out **to embrace me**."

On his five-month sentence for tax evasion (*Sunday Conversation, 1991*):

"I paid 94 percent of my taxes, which is usually good enough. But you have to pay all your taxes. I've learned from this. I tried to pay 110 percent this year, but they wouldn't let me."

On having his suspension lifted (*Up Close, 1995*):

"**I've kept my mouth shut** – I don't whine. **I've politicked for the Hall of Fame** for 24 years as a player; **I don't think I need to** go out and politick for it now."

Mike Tyson on Mike Tyson

From *SportsCenter*, 1989:

"I'm the **best in the world**, even though a lot of you **don't like to hear it**. In fact, I'm the best, you know what I mean? Sometimes **I don't want to believe it myself**, but it's the truth. **I'm the best**."

From *Up Close*, 1989:

{ "I'm totally in control of the situation in the ring. There is a certain amount of moderation as far as discipline is concerned. When you're in the ring, it's like a diagram: everything's written out in your head and everything's planned out to do." }

From *SportsCenter*, 1990:

"We make the monsters. **We create the monsters that we are.** Directly or indirectly, somehow we do it. We have **no one to blame for ourselves.** I can't feel sorry and **I can't expect anyone to feel sorry** for me, because whatever happened in my life, more or less, **I created it**."

From *Up Close, 1991*:

"My main concern in life in general isn't what any commentator says, my main concern is what my peers think of me, other fighters, because they know what it takes to reach the pinnacle of success."

From *"The Lost Champion," Outside the Lines, 1992*:

"I believe that a lot of people **want to see me self-destruct**. They want to see me **one day with handcuffs** and walking to the police cars, **going to jail** like you see Marlon Brando's son. **My objective in life** and my sole success **is that I'm successful**, that **I'm not in jail**, that **I'm not in Brownsville anymore** and **I beat all the odds."**

From *"Tyson, the Return," Outside the Lines, 1995*:

["Mike Tyson is actually like a cold, businesslike killer."]

From *Up Close Primetime, 1997*:

"We need to show our heart, our determination. We're there to spill our blood. If we think we're there just to look good and gain fans, no, that's not it. We're there to suffer. We're there to die."

CHAPTER 10

Here I am, in print, assailing those, in print, who smugly contend that "television sports journalism" is an oxymoron/opiate for an industry paying billions for events that it presents with the subtlety of a Las Vegas chorus line. Well, as we used to say in Jersey, *I gotch your oxymoron right here*. We at ESPN have considerable time for observation and conversation. There's that moment, as you're conducting an interview, when you say to yourself, Did he really say that? Producers call them soundbites. I prefer to think of them as windows on the soul. –BOB LEY

"Coincidence? Or **conspiracy?**"

Sports in Black and White

Sean Jones *("Inside Titletown U.S.A.," Outside the Lines, 1996)*:

"The pressure of being black in Green Bay is no different than being white in Harlem."

Joe Black, on being denied the opportunity to play major league baseball because he was black *(ESPN.SportsZone, 1996)*:

{ "That made me hurt. And when you hurt, you hate, and I hated all white people and I hated this country because I couldn't understand how you could be an American and not be able to play the American pastime." }

Don King, on his use of the word nigger *("Portraits in Black and White," Outside the Lines, 1992)*:

"For the **simple reason** that it invoked the **type of passion** and **emotion** that would **bring discussion**. You are a nigger till you die. Nigger is **the beginning and the end**. You got Negro, Afro-American, colored, blacks, macaroons, mulattos.If you are a poor nigger, **you're a poor nigger**. But I've taken nigger and **changed it around** and **made it a positive word**. If you're a rich nigger, **you're a rich nigger**."

Jim Brown (*"Portraits in Black and White," Outside the Lines, 1992*):

"As you go into the six figures, it's going to be very comfortable being an imitation white man."

Reggie White, on white people's perception of him (*Sunday Conversation, 1993*):

"They don't think of me as a black man. They think of me as an athlete who's made it, so they put me on their level."

NFL agent **Leigh Steinberg** (*Up Close, 1997*):

"Professional sports is one of the few areas of this society where white and black people interact as real human beings, not stereotypes. They're with each other day and night in some situations. It's not five talking heads on *Washington Week in Review* – these are people down in the trenches together."

Robin Roberts (*ESPN.SportsZone, 1996*):

"People see my gender first, then my ethnic background, so I honestly can't say it's been more difficult being a black woman. It's hard just being a woman, period, in sports."

Art Modell, on minority coaches in the NFL
(*"Portraits in Black and White," Outside the Lines, 1992*):

"I'll wager that for every job opening there are at least two or three black candidates based on Dennis Green's success. Not because owners feel an obligation to be evenhanded, to be progressive. They want to win. The owners in this league would sell their wives into slavery if they could, if they can win a football game. You're looking at one. I'm not exempt from that."

Tony Dungy (*Sunday Conversation, 1997*):

"Everyone has an idea of what their **head coach** is going to be. Some owners want an **outgoing guy**, they want a **tough guy**, they want a **disciplinarian**. Some guys want an **offensive guy**. Some guys want an **older guy** or a **younger guy**. And I think a lot of people, in their mind, their vision of the head coach is **white**."

Joe Black, on black baseball players failing to acknowledge
Jackie Robinson's legacy (*ESPN.SportsZone, 1997*):

"Many blacks, young and old, don't understand the contributions of blacks to this country. All they think is that we play sports and sing songs."

Hank Aaron, on the aftermath of the racial abuse he had
faced pursuing Babe Ruth's home run record (*"Breaking the Line:
Jackie Robinson's Legacy," Outside the Lines, 1997*):

"It was the **hardest** thing. I don't talk about it that
much. It had **taken a piece of my life** with it. Rather
than being happy, it was **a sad moment**."

Mike Krzyzewski (*"It's a Mad, Mad, Mad, Mad Game," Outside the Lines, 1995*):
"Certainly we **should have** a lot of coaches who are **African-Americans**. However, **don't tell me** as a Polish coach that I **can't coach** a kid from the **inner city. I can coach anybody**."

Jackie Robinson's widow, **Rachel,** on what progress her husband felt had been made over his lifetime (*"Breaking the Line: Jackie Robinson's Legacy," Outside the Lines, 1997*):

"His level of optimism diminished over time. As a younger person, he still thought that with hard work and skill and being a good person one could get integrated into the society. He soon found out that that was not the case."

Outside the Law

Allen Iverson, after being arrested for speeding and possession of a gun and marijuana, on how he would explain it to his daughter (*Sunday Conversation, 1997*):

"Daddy made a **mistake**."

Nick Bakay (*Talk 2, 1995*):

"Seattle Seahawks running back Chris Warren has been charged with assaulting a woman outside a nightclub. Add this to Brian Blades facing manslaughter charges, Dennis Erickson's DWI arrest and Lamar Smith's pending vehicular assault trial. Look for the Seahawks to fill their final roster slot with a bail bondsman and ask some players to restructure their deals so the club can fit Johnny Cochran's retainer under the salary cap."

Retired Trailblazer **Michael Harper**, on the rash of run-ins with the law among his former teammates (*"Sports under Arrest" Outside the Lines, 1997*):

"Who would you invite on the current Portland Trailblazer team to come and speak to the school where your kid goes?"

Tom Osborne, when questioned about refusing to suspend Lawrence Phillips after an assault charge while the running back was at Nebraska (*Up Close Primetime, 1996*):

{ "The better question would have been **what would you have done with Lawrence Phillips** if he'd been your son, because essentially that's the role I'm cast in. **I've done what I would do for my own son.**" }

Bob Ley (*"Sports Under Arrest," Outside the Lines, 1997*):

"Teams consider 'character' when drafting players, but fans seem to want more. They already feel disconnected from millionaire players, and they want to feel that values have a place in this discussion; that bad actions have consequences, as in their own lives; that, along with the vital principles of civil rights and union contracts, there is another concept, at least as important, called The Right Thing To Do. This sports industry that exists at the pleasure of the consumer dollar ought to figure out what that Right Thing is. And then Just Do It."

Charles Barkley (*Up Close Primetime, 1997*):

"We are held to such **a higher standard**, and we should be.
But **come on, don't go crazy**. Don't make us out to be
Public Enemy No.1 because we do **one thing wrong**.
Athletes do 99 percent good things and one percent bad things,
and **people never let you forget** about that one percent."

Paul Molitor, on why society is so forgiving of athletes
(*"Sports Under Arrest," Outside the Lines, 1997*):

"The fact that it is so difficult to replace a
certain talent **at this level** makes people
put **blinders on** sometimes in order to get
those people **back out here** to perform."

Christian Peter, after being released by the Patriots for
a variety of legal troubles (*SportsWeekly, 1996*):

"Christian Peter is the **victim** – I'm not
**Attila the Hun. I'm not some
barbarian** that runs around going crazy.
Like I said, **to know me is to love
me**, and not to know and just **believe
what you read** and believe what you
hear, **that's not fair to me**. It would
be nice if you took the chance to **get to
know** the **real Christian Peter."**

Barry Switzer, explaining why there was a gun in a bag that he had attempted to carry onto an airplane while traveling with the Cowboys (*SportsCenter*, 1997):

"I had nine houseguests this weekend. Three of them happened to be an 11-year-old, a 10-year-old and a 2-year-old. I walked into my bedroom with them all present and I saw my gun lying on the bed. I sat my bag down that I travel with and I put the gun in the bag with full intentions of putting it back in the drawer beside the bed where I keep it. This morning I got up at 8 a.m. and dressed in the same Bermuda shorts that I left with, threw on another T-shirt and threw all my toiletries in that same bag, and went to the airport in a rush to catch a 9 a.m. plane. I put my bag in security, went through security, wondered why my bag had stopped. I'm waiting, having a conversation with people, and I look up. There are two police officers standing beside me and they looked at me with a serious look. All of a sudden I realized, Oh my God, I didn't take the pistol out of my bag."

Wilt Chamberlain, on his claim in his autobiography that he slept with over 20,000 women (*Sunday Conversation, 1993*):

"I never assumed that anyone would **make so much out of a statement** of **a number**."

Comedian **Elayne Boosler**, on Wilt Chamberlain's claim (*Up Close, 1991*):

"Twenty thousand different women and where was I? Odds like that and I still don't win the lottery."

Wilt Chamberlain, on abstinence (*Sunday Conversation, 1993*):

"I can **believe** in it. I don't know **how long** I can **sustain** it."

A more evolved **Wilt Chamberlain** (*Up Close, 1995*):

"For all **you men** that think having **1,000 different women** is cool, I have found that having **one woman 1,000 different times** is really the **way to go**."

The Story Behind the Story

Jayson Williams, to his fellow NBA players in the wake of the
Latrell Sprewell incident (*SportsCenter, 1997*):

"You've got to **clean up the big shorts.** You've got to **clean up the cursing.** This is not the **playground,** it's the **NBA.** The playground may have **got you here,** but if you keep acting like you're **on the playground,** all of us are **out of a job** because the **people will stop buying tickets.**"

Arnold Schwarzenegger, on his steroid use (*Up Close, 1984*):

"I was one of those people who **did it really wisely** and **under a doctor's supervision.** I didn't really see much difference one way or the other, but then **maybe I didn't take enough** where you would have seen a difference. What is **more important right now** is to **avoid drugs,** because drugs are only **a very temporary thing** in sports. **What is permanent** is that we **train our mind.**"

Sean Jones, on painkiller abuse in the NFL (*NFL Countdown, 1996*):

"The **best question** for me is if you said, Hey, there's **a game on the line**—would you **take painkillers** to **get through it?** And without hestitation I'd answer, **Of course, I would.**"

Bennie Blades, on the repercussions of several incidents involving high-profile athletes and domestic violence (*NFL Countdown, 1996*):

"It's going to be a lot harder for us to get out of trouble now than it was three years ago. Three years ago, you smacked your girl around, people say maybe she asked for it. Nowadays, whether she asked for it or not, they're going to haul you off."

WBO Mini-flyweight champion **Alex Sanchez**, on Wil Cordero being charged with assaulting his wife (*SportsCenter, 1997*).

"A lot of cases happen like this because the **woman doesn't want to accept the rules** that are **imposed by the husband**. That's why sometimes it gets to the **extreme** where the husband abuses on her. I'm not saying always, I'm saying **almost always** the **woman is at fault**."

Don King, on corruption in boxing (*Talk 2, 1994*):

"I don't know anything about the corruption. If there is any, you have to find it somewhere else. All I am going to do is to continue to perform in this great land called America. I love this country. I love what it stands for."

Michael Jordan, on allegations that he was suspended by the NBA for gambling (*Sunday Conversation, 1995*):

"There were **no penalties**; I didn't do **anything wrong** in terms of **the gambling situation**. I walked away because **I chose to walk away**. **When I walked back**, I walked back because I **chose to** walk back, **not** because **my time was expired**."

Chicago Tribune columnist **Bob Greene**, on the connection between Michael Jordan's dream of being a baseball player and his father's murder (*"Jordan's Dream Spring," Outside the Lines, 1994*):

"This is a grieving that has been completely internal. Michael says when he was six years old his dad put him on a baseball field. And his dad was the first person to want him to be a baseball player. It has to do with Michael and it has to do with Michael's father, and it doesn't have very much to do with the rest of the world."

Late Canadian actor **John Candy**, on sprinter Ben Johnson
losing his gold medal for steroid use (*Up Close, 1991*):

"**All** of our **hopes** and **dreams** rested on
the shoulders of **Ben Johnson**, and then he crossed
the **finish line** setting the **world record**, and
then he **had to go to the washroom**, and then
it **was all over.** If he just would have said, **I don't
have to go now** – that's **all** he had to say."

CHAPTER 11

Once upon a time, a certain parentally inclined *SportsCenter* anchor thought it would be a great idea to say "He's no Beanie Baby" over a highlight, using the popular toy to say an athlete's not soft (which is good). Not so the reaction to the phrase (which was bad). Sure, there'd be viewers who wouldn't know a Beanie Baby from Beano Cook. But then there were the few who got the reference but missed the point, thinking I was bashing the guy instead of giving his hard play a boost. The moral? Even when you go out of your way to talk nice, plenty will still think you're talking trash. —LINDA COHN

"He's no Beanie Baby."

"**AMERICA:** YOUR MOMMA'S SO DUMB SHE LOOKED AT THE UMBILICAL CORD AND SAID, **LOOK, IT COMES WITH CABLE!** **JAPAN:** THE MOST-HONORED ANCESTORS OF YOUR MATRIARCH **BESMIRCHED** THE **SEASON OF THE ORANGE BLOSSOM**."

Chris Webber (*Talk 2, 1994*):

"The biggest trash talker that ever lived was Larry Bird. Good players just have that walk, that cockiness. When we're on the court, I am not a great person. I'm trying to beat you and I'm trying to mentally harm you."

Kareem Abdul-Jabbar, on being mistaken for Wilt Chamberlain (*Sunday Conversation, 1991*):

"**I'm not that clumsy.**"

Howard Cosell, on Mike Tyson (*SportsCenter, 1992*):

"**He's a common criminal** who's getting what he deserves. He's finished, washed up, deserves to be, period. **He's a thug.**"

Barry Bonds (*Up Close, 1996*):

{ "If you want to, embrace me. If you don't, don't. Those who stopped calling me because I ain't at the ESPY Awards and the music awards and everything else, it's fine with me. **I know exactly who you are**. So then when I do come back out and put up one of them good years and hopefully win that fourth MVP award, **you'll be back**. But see, my phone's off the hook . . . beep . . . beep . . . beep . . . beep." }

Buddy Ryan, on why he threw a punch at fellow Oilers coach Kevin Gilbride (*Up Close, 1996*):

"He came after me. I mean, I called him a **High School Charlie**, and he came after me."

Jeremy Roenick, after Avalanche goalie Patrick Roy said he'd have no problem stopping the then-Blackhawk on a penalty shot (*SportsCenter, 1996*):

"I just want to know where he was in Game 3 – probably **getting his jock out of the rafters** of the United Center."

Patrick Roy's comeback (*SportsCenter, 1996*):

"I can't really hear what Jeremy said because **I have my two Stanley Cup rings plugged in my ears**."

George Foreman (*SportsCenter, 1992*):

"I'm going to go to Baskin-Robbins and **I'm going to eat every flavor of ice cream** in the world. And **when you start pushing and shoving me**, you're going to have to **push and shove a whole franchise.**"

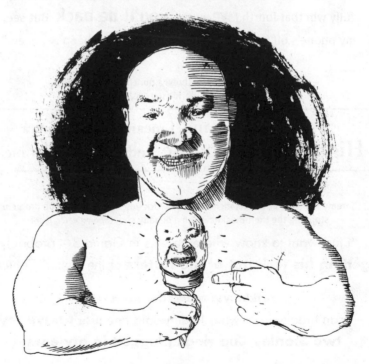

Michael Irvin, after the Cowboys were beaten by the Panthers
in the NFC playoffs (*SportsCenter, 1996*):

"We're not going to the Super Bowl, **we're going home**. We let somebody borrow our house last year, that's what we did. Now I'm going home and I'm going to make sure. **I'm going to check the lease** – see if they left it dirty, see if they cleaned up behind themselves. **But where we are going is home**. Period."

Horace Grant (*Talk 2, 1994*):

"A skunk kills itself by the publicity it gives itself. In the long run, **Charles Barkley's mouth is going to catch up with him.**"

Bryan Cox (*Sportsmanship in the '90s Town Meeting, 1997*):

"I'm a guy who **likes to talk trash** – mamas, babies, wives. The **only** thing I **won't touch** is if you have **someone who's sick**."

Kicker **Kevin Butler**, after being replaced by Carlos Huerta on the Bears (*Up Close, 1996*):

"They can pick the kicker that kicks it longer, stronger, higher, faster and with more accuracy, or else they can pick Carlos."

Barry Bonds, on whether he's a better ballplayer than Ken Griffey Jr. (*Up Close Primetime, 1996*):

"I'm a better left fielder. [Pause.] We hit the same amount of home runs; the averages are about the same. He's a better center fielder; I'm a better left fielder. I outrun him. That's about all I do more than Ken Griffey Jr."

David Justice, responding to people who say he was crazy for divorcing Halle Berry (*Sunday Conversation, 1996*):

"Beauty is only **skin deep**."

Dan Patrick, after reporting that 38 percent of the people who used Dennis Rodman's name as an alias when ordering from Domino's Pizza greeted the driver wearing a dress (*SportsCenter, 1997*):

"It's none of my business what **Keith Olbermann does when he's not working.**"

Brett Hull (*Sunday Conversation, 1992*):

"I'm not **dumb enough** to be a goalie."

Mavericks GM **Don Nelson**, on trading away Jason Kidd, Jimmy Jackson and Jamal Mashburn (*SportsCenter, 1997*):

"Just because these [expletive] players are complaining about the coach doesn't mean anything. They've complained about every coach since they've been here. That's why I got rid of them. [Expletive] babies. And you can quote me on that."

Brett Haber, on Goran Ivanisevic at the 1996 Grand Slam Cup (*SportsCenter, 1996*):

"Goran's still sporting that horrendous Pebbles Flintstone, samurai hairdo thing. Quite frankly, it's just not a good look."

Herschel Walker (*Sunday Conversation, 1992*):

"When you start talking about measuring my heart, you're talking about not just me but my family. It's not football anymore, it's facing me as a man. I don't think too many men can face me and say, Oh Herschel, your heart is not in the game. Because I would guarantee you I would knock his head off."

Bobby Knight, on the media (*Sunday Conversation, 1994*):

"They ought to take all you television people and build a [expletive] island for you, and put these writers in a cave under the island."

Rick Pitino (*Sunday Conversation, 1996*):

"You know the camera is on you when you're going to say something to a player and you want to come across positively. So what I do is clap, smile and say, That's all right, I'm going to kill ya. Next time out you're dead."

Tony **Bruno**, interviewing President Bill Clinton during Arkansas'
NCAA Championship run (*ESPN Radio Network*, *1995*):

"Ladies and gentleman — the **President** of the United States. **This is not a joke.** People might think that because I like to clown around a lot here that **we're pulling a fast one** on the American public — but we're not. I appreciate you joining us."

President Bill Clinton (*ESPN Radio Network*, *1995*):

"I'm glad to do it. And I'm glad to be in a conversation where **the American public** think **someone else** is **pulling a fast one** on them **instead** of the **President.**"

Fearsome Foursome defensive end **Deacon Jones**, on inventing trash talk (*Up Close*, *1996*):

"I WAS THE **ORIGINATOR OF SMACK**. SOME GUYS **RATTLE** WITH SMACK; WITH OTHER GUYS IT **ROLLS RIGHT OFF** THEIR SHOULDERS LIKE NOTHING. **LIKE JOHNNY UNITAS, IT DIDN'T BOTHER HIM ONE BIT**. IF YOU WEREN'T RUSHING HIM, HE WAS GOING TO **RUN THE SCOREBOARD** UP ON YOU, **SIMPLE AS THAT**."

CHAPTER 12

If your father is 5'8" and your mother is 5'3", you can forget about being a center in the NBA. But while a winning ticket in the genetic lottery can put you in the game, it's the emotional legacy that can make or break you. Perhaps the greatest athlete of our time, Michael Jordan, had a special relationship with his father, who was murdered in 1993. So much so that after the Bulls won their fourth title three years later, Jordan wept uncontrollably, not for what he had won, but for what he had lost. For Jordan, family matters. It matters most of all. —BILL PIDTO

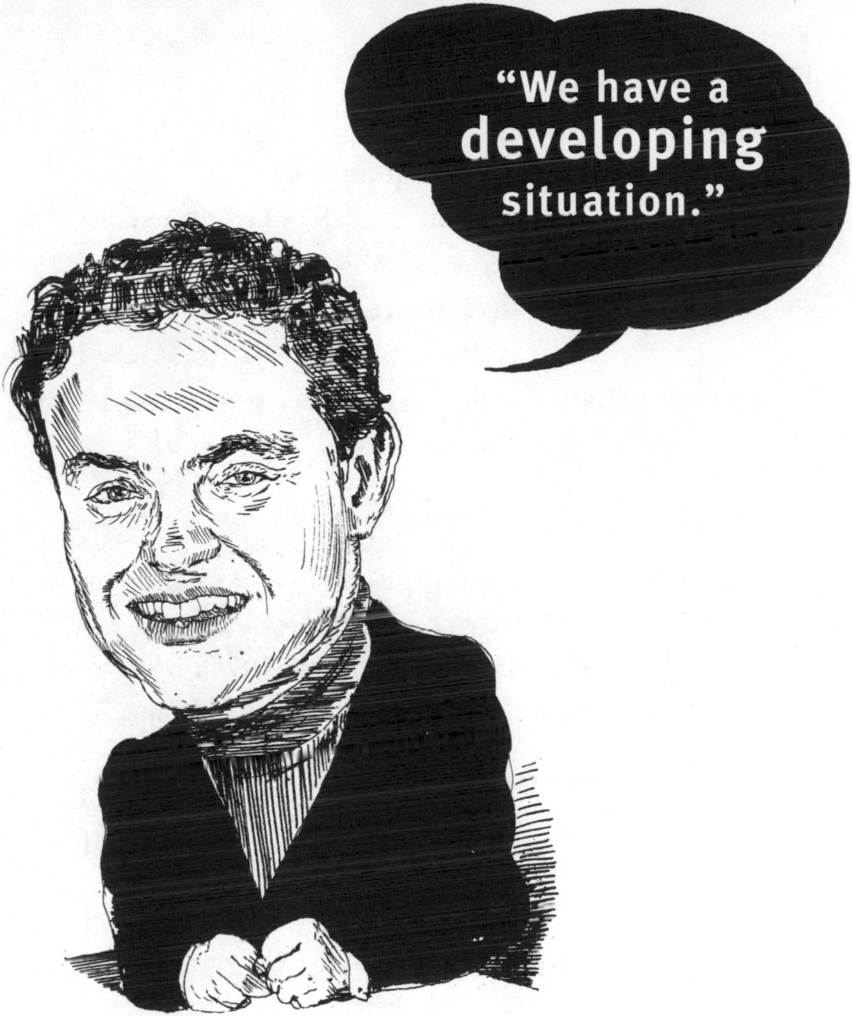
"We have a developing situation."

George Brett (*Up Close*, *1994*):

"In 1980, I missed hitting .400 by five hits and the first thing my father says is, 'You mean to tell me you couldn't get five more blankety-blank hits?' But that's the way he was, because if he knew I was ever satisfied with what I did, my performance would have not continued to be as good."

Tiger Woods, repeating the inspirational words of his father the night before the last round of the Masters (*Sunday Conversation*, *1997*):

"Tomorrow when you go out there, it's going to be **one of the hardest rounds** of your life, but if you **just be yourself**, **stay cool**, it will be one of the **most rewarding rounds** of your life."

Earl Woods, on why Tiger embraced him after winning the Masters (*ESPN Radio Network*, *1997*):

"He doesn't have a **wife,** he doesn't even have a **girlfriend,** so the **only people** he has to call on **is me.**"

Phil Mickelson, on whether his father had trained him like
Earl Woods trained Tiger (*ESPN.SportsZone, 1997*):

"No, my dad was fun."

Chi Chi Rodriguez (*Up Close, 1994*):

"My father was a **wonderful man**.
He was **a very poor man** and he'd
never complain about nothing, but he
was rich **when it came to love**.
He used to wear long boots, and **every
night** when he came home from work,
one of us would have to take his boots off,
one would bring hot water and
the soap, and **we would wash his
feet**. Then my sister would take a razor
blade and **cut his corns**. When a
man can **have his kids do that**,
he is **a very wealthy man**."

Michael Jordan, on the aftermath of his father's murder (*Sunday Conversation, 1995*):

{ "I had to build up strength within myself
to pursue life after James Jordan. That was the
toughest part of coming back and playing." }

Joe Paterno (*Up Close, 1991*):

"My father was dead broke, but he came up with $20 bucks a month for me to go to a Jesuit high school because he felt that strongly about education. My mom and dad never went to a movie, they hardly ever went out, and then I went to Brown University."

Shaquille O'Neal, on the impact his stepfather had on him
(*"Shaq's Sudden Impact," Outside the Lines, 1993*):

"I was a **bad kid**, and **he put it to me a lot**. And, like some of those kids around here, that's what they need, somebody to put it to them. Discipline. **I have a lot of discipline**, and if it wasn't for him, **I probably wouldn't be here** talking to you."

Grant Hill, accepting the ESPY for Male College Basketball
Performer of the Year (*ESPY Awards, 1995*):

"I'd like to thank my Dad for not allowing me to play football when I was little."

Grant Hill, on his memory of his father, Calvin, as a Cowboy (*Sunday Conversation, 1994*):

"I remember him being old and sitting on the bench and not playing a lot and I was like, He's not that good."

Like Father, Like Son

Cal Ripken Sr., on what he admires about his son
(*"A Rip of Games," Outside the Lines, 1995*):

"He didn't start out in baseball **to break Lou Gehrig's streak**. This all came about because **a man goes to his job** and **works every day**. That's what you want."

Ken Griffey Sr., on the benefits of having a millionaire
son at dinnertime (*SportsCenter, 1996*):

"Who do you think is buying? Do you think I am buying? The tip and all the other stuff goes to Junior."

NBA All-Star dunk champ **Brent Barry** (*SportsCenter, 1996*):

> "A lot of **people ask me** if it was **my father** who taught me to dunk. Come on. **It was my mother**."

Isiah Thomas (*Up Close, 1992*):

"When **I left college**, my mother **made me sign a contract** stating that **I would go back and finish school**. I went back and finished, and **I say that to all the kids** when I am talking to them because I just don't stand up and **preach education** when I don't have one. **I graduated on Mother's Day.** We were playing the Atlanta Hawks and **I couldn't go and get my degree**, so **my mother** walked down the aisle **and she got it**. When my mother grew up, they **didn't allow blacks to be educated**, so she got a third grade education and everything else **she had to learn on her own**. That was my way of saying, **Okay, Mom, you graduated also**."

Larry Bird (*SportsCenter, 1992*):

"My mother worked a lot of hours. She always worked double shifts. We used to take her pay check and buy all of the food, and Father's check and pay most of the bills, and we barely just got by. I think that's the way everyone should grow up."

Mike Tyson, on his mother's reaction to the delinquency of his youth (*Sunday Conversation, 1992*):

"One day I gave her a bunch of money and said, 'Oh, Ma, don't even ask me where I got it from. Just take it and buy something.' She was so hurt that I would go that way. She was embarrassed that I was that way."

Announcer **Vin Scully** (*Up Close, 1990*):

"My mother was Irish, red-haired and unemotional. She was not the kind of woman to put her arms around me. Because of that I learned to be unemotional as a broadcaster."

Lawrence Taylor (*SportsCenter, 1992*):

"I realized I was special when I was young and my mother walked into the house and she spanked the other two kids and didn't get me."

[*the real challenge*]

CHAPTER 13

We are constantly bombarded by numbers. Sports-speak is all about statistics and final scores and salary caps and salaries with no caps. We are so immersed in numbers that they often come to represent an individual – give me a number, I'll give you a name. Yet behind those figures, beyond the dollar signs, is a person who eats, sleeps and bleeds just like you and I do. Money can open one's eyes to the finer things in life, but it also blinds us. Athletes are as vulnerable to pain, tragedy, crime and punishment as the guy driving the team bus. –KARL RAVECH

Jim Valvano, accepting the Arthur Ashe Award for Courage (*ESPY Awards, 1993*):

"Cancer can take away all my physical abilities. It cannot touch **my mind**, it cannot touch **my heart** and it cannot touch **my soul**. These three things are going **to carry on forever**."

Arthur Ashe, on whether contracting AIDS had shaken his faith (*Up Close, 1992*):

"There is a very strong affinity between the black experience and Jesus Christ: He was poor, he was homeless, he was a member of a despised minority, he was persecuted. When he was on the cross he said, 'Why have you forsaken me?' It's a little bit like asking, Why me at such an early age? And I think it's really the wrong question to ask, because why not me?"

Ernie Irvan, on returning to racing after injuring his left eye in a 1992 crash that put him in a coma (*Sunday Conversation, 1994*):

"I can outdrive most of them guys **with one eye** anyway."

Kirby Puckett, on when he first realized he had eye problems (*Sunday Conversation, 1996*):

"I got up, kind of shook my head. My wife was getting something out of the dryer and I looked and I said, 'Babe, I can't see you.'"

Arnold Palmer, on why he chose to treat his prostate cancer with surgery (*SportsCenter, 1996*):

"It's **like having two trees out in front of you** and you have **a five-iron in your hand** about 189 yards from the green. You know, **you pitch it out or hit a wedge,** or **you can hit it between the trees** and if it gets it done, **you're there.**"

Mickie Krzyzewski, on convincing her husband, Mike, that he needed to take a break from coaching at Duke (*Sunday Conversation, 1995*):

"He looked like he was 80 years old. I told him him to meet me at the hospital instead of going to practice. I said, 'Michael, I've never said this to you in our whole married life, but it's me or basketball.'"

Jimmy Connors, on his blue-collar roots (*Up Close*, 1992):

"Tennis was given to me **not** to become a great player and a world champion. Tennis was given to me to **keep me off the street** corners of East St. Louis."

["I came to the ballpark today and
**took the chewing tobacco out of
my locker** and **put it in the trash can**.
I'm not going to touch the stuff. I've chewed
tobacco for a long time and I enjoy it, but
life to me is a little more important
than sticking tobacco in your mouth."]

Skier **Diana Golden** (*Up Close, 1991*):

"I have one leg, and wishing it back isn't
going to bring it back. I can accept the situation and,
in my case, I can embrace the situation and say, Okay,
this is it, what am I going to do with it? Then you
see that you have that choice every day in your
life with everything – it's not just having
one leg: Now here's the situation I am in, it's really
crummy, but let me embrace it, let me work with it, let
me take something positive out of it."

Former Packer **Lionel Aldridge**, on being homeless (*Up Close, 1988*):

"The absolute **bottom of the world** is living on the street. When you're on the street you **aren't in a mood to listen to empathy,** because that **doesn't do a thing for you.**"

Lyle Alzado, on contracting cancer from long-term steroid use (*Up Close, 1991*):

"I don't want to die, however trite that sounds. For 16 years, if I had to do that – take the steroids, the growth hormone for my comeback and all the other stuff that I did – I wouldn't give up my life for it. The kids walking on the beach that have their bodies built by steroids, the athletes that compete in pro football, pro basketball, pro baseball, I don't think they should have to make the choice. There should be no choice."

Bob Ojeda, on surviving a boating accident that killed two Indian teammates (*Sunday Conversation, 1994*):

"I don't want to FOOL AROUND with FEAR – it could be bigger if it wants."

Gail Devers, on battling Grave's Disease (*Up Close, 1996*):

"I DEFINITELY BELIEVE THAT WITH **ALL THAT I'VE GONE THROUGH** IN MY LIFE WITH MY INJURIES AND ILLNESSES **I'M A STRONGER PERSON**. I'M MORE DETERMINED AND **I DON'T THINK THERE IS ANYTHING THAT I CAN'T ENCOUNTER OR CONQUER** AFTER WHAT I'VE GONE THROUGH."

John Daly, on how he justified his drinking (*SportsCenter, 1997*):

"I got to a point where I thought I was a better player drinking . . . There were times when I saw three balls. I just made sure I hit the middle one . . . Hey, I played some great golf where I went out and got just as smashed as when I played bad golf. It's not about good play or bad play, it's about the disease and what it can do to you."

Boxer **Bobby Czyz,** on standing up to his abusive father (*Up Close, 1992*):

"On my 18th birthday, I said to my father, 'I am a man now. What I want for my birthday is for you never to hit my mother again.' He looked me dead in my face and said, 'I cannot do that. I cannot give you that, but as often as I hit her, it would have been more if you didn't ask.'"

Dwight Gooden, on recovering from drug addiction (*Up Close Primetime, 1997*):

"The foremost thing in my life now is staying sober and clean from day to day, because without that, there's no baseball, there's no kids, there's no wife, there's no anything."

John Daly (*Sunday Conversation, 1992*):

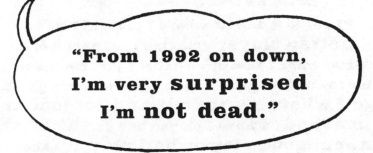

"From 1992 on down, I'm very surprised I'm not dead."

Cris Carter (*NFL Countdown, 1996*):

"When I **look in the mirror** I see **an alcoholic**, I see a person who is chemically dependent — and it helps me. **I don't live a life in fear. I live a life in victory.** That's my message to a lot of kids."

"It's strange about ignorance. You go out robbing people and mugging people and you don't know it's wrong. One night the police started chasing me and I thought, Why are they chasing me? I didn't hurt anyone; I just stole a guy's wallet.

And they were closing in on me and I ran near my house to hide. I covered myself from head to toe in mud because I thought they were going to send the dogs in to sniff me out. It was then that I realized I was a crook. That was the last time I ever stole something. I didn't want to be a criminal, but it took me covering myself with mud to realize what I had become."

193

Former Patriot **Darryl Stingley**, who was paralyzed in
a game in 1978 (*SportsCenter, 1992*):

"Very often **when I'm watching football**
games, it seems as if on **every play** somebody
should or could be injured. **It's like they're all
walking on grenades** out there because it's
that type of game in the '90s."

Mickey Mantle (*Up Close, 1986*):

"I've always felt that I burned
the candle at both ends."

Umpire **Steve Palermo**, who was shot and paralyzed while preventing a robbery,
accepting the Arthur Ashe Award for Courage (*ESPY Awards, 1994*) :

"What we did that evening in Dallas, hopefully
Arthur would approve of. Because it was out of
respect for those two women. Nobody has the right
to play God with a gun. They don't have
the right to wave that pistol to hurt, maim,
paralyze or take somebody's life."

Then-Bruin **Sheldon Kennedy,** revealing that he'd been sexually abused
by respected Junior hockey coach Graham James (*SportsCenter, 1997*):

"He took THE YOUTH right out of me. My years from 14 until now have been A FOG."

Sheldon Kennedy, describing the first assault (*SportsCenter, 1997*):

"**It was pitch black** and the windows were all taped up and **I couldn't see what he was doing**. I heard him go into the closet, then he came back, sat on the bed and **he had a shotgun in his hand**. From that point on, **he had me**."

Sheldon Kennedy, on how he feels about Graham James today (*SportsCenter, 1997*):

"I wish I could **invent a pill** that you could give him that would **screw him up mentally** like I was for **twice the amount of years** and then have to have **him deal with life**."

CHAPTER 14

How do you describe the indescribable? When something catches your eye, you've already seen it before you realize what you're looking at. When you hear good music, you start tapping your feet without thinking about it. You can't explain it, you can't describe it, but you'll feel it when you're there. And when an athlete is in The Zone, there's nothing better. It's Michael Jordan at the buzzer, Tiger Woods at the Masters, John Elway leading the comeback. It's the very definition of "Wow!" –CHRIS MYERS

"That deserves a Wow!"

Magic Johnson (*Up Close, 1990*):

"My motto is this: Just wake up and have a good day, have a good time, and no matter what goes wrong, turn that into something good. Still come out smiling, still come out having a good time."

Frank Robinson, on being a great clutch hitter (*Up Close Primetime, 1996*):

"**Tony Perez covered it**. He says, 'Frank, the way I look at it, especially **with the bases loaded, the pitcher is in trouble, not me**.'"

U.S. Olympic softball pitcher **Lisa Fernandez**
(*"Women & Sports at the Crossroads," Outside the Lines, 1997*):

"It's just amazing to see how people now perceive us as athletes and realize that it's okay for us to bleed, it's okay for us to sweat and to cry and to be angry and to be frustrated and to show aggression and still be considered as females when we walk off the field or walk off the surface."

Dennis Rodman, on his role as a rebounder (*ESPN Radio Network, 1995*):

"I'm the gravedigger – I put the body in the hole."

Dave Stewart, on his attitude toward pitching (*Sunday Conversation, 1993*):

"The hitter is not a factor. What's a factor is if **I make a mistake** or not, and **I'm not willing** to make that mistake **to let him beat me.**"

Marshall Faulk (*Sunday Conversation, 1992*):

"It just seems like sometimes when I have the ball, other people are moving in slow motion."

Dick Trickle (*ESPN.SportsZone, 1997*).

"Driving is mentally like leaning over the edge of the cliff and seeing how far you can lean over without falling off."

Nolan Ryan, on the secret to his longevity (*Sunday Conversation, 1993*):

"**Genetics**, and that **I didn't sustain any injuries** that took away from **my natural ability**."

John Elway (*Up Close Primetime, 1996*):

"Each year, **the older I get**, the **harder I work** because it takes **that much more** each week to come back. The hard work has really helped me, but **the bottom line?** God gave me **a football body**."

Roy Campanella (*Up Close, 1986*):

"You can **play forever** as long as you **keep** that **little boy in you**."

Mike Piazza (*Up Close Primetime, 1997*):

"I'd rather be **the best-hitting catcher** for **10 years** than **just another first baseman** or another position **for 15 or 20**."

Michael Jordan (*Sunday Conversation, 1992*):

"I've never been a vocal leader. I lead with my play. My play does all my talking. I go out every night and play like I'm playing the last game."

Gordie Howe (*Talk 2, 1994*):

"If you **give a lot every shift,** then win or lose you go home and **sleep exceptionally well** – and the **best-rested athlete plays the best**."

Deion Sanders (*Up Close*, 1997):

"I keep my body in shape and well conditioned. I know my game. I study my game. I have a Ph.D. in my game."

Jerry Rice (*Up Close*, 1996):

"When I first came into the league, I wanted to be the best receiver to ever play the game, but now I would like to be the best football player to ever put a uniform on."

Bill Walsh, after Jerry Rice's attempt to come back after major knee surgery resulted in another injury (*Up Close*, 1997):

{ "People lost track of the fact that, as great as he is, Jerry Rice is human." }

Mike Schmidt (*Up Close Primetime*, 1996):

"The feeling of running around the bases is one of the great feelings in sports. It would be like Jerry Rice catching the ball on the 40 and having nobody near him. You pretty much can do whatever you want, right?"

ABL guard **Debbie Black**, the first pro woman to score a quadruple-double, on the advantages of being 5'3" (*ESPN.SportsZone, 1997*):

"People tend to **take me lightly** because of **my height** and I use that against them. I'm **lower to the ground** and **closer to the ball**, and I try to get a lot of steals **by being sneaky.**"

Cal Ripken Jr., on how he maintained The Streak (*"A Rip of Games," Outside the Lines, 1995*):

> "It could be 50 percent luck, 50 percent persistance, durability, stubbornness and who knows what else. Probably the most important factor is that I love to play."

Tennessee coach **Pat Summitt** (*ESPN.SportsZone, 1997*):

"We're in the '90s and, yes, **kids are different**, but something that has **remained constant** in my 23 years of coaching is that student athletes **want discipline**."

Tim Duncan (*Sunday Conversation, 1997*):

"The **time** when there is **no one there to feel sorry for you** or **to cheer you** is **when a player is made**."

Dennis Rodman (*Up Close Primetime, 1997*):

"**I like entertaining people** every day. **That's my high**. That's my blow right there. If people think I do crack, hey, we can do a blood test right now, any day you want. **You'll find nothing** in my system **but good love** and **kindness** and **understanding**."

Brett Favre (*Up Close Primetime, 1997*):

"I go and **I dive** and **I block** and **I throw it** underhand. I'm in the **weight room** in the morning, I go to **extra meetings**, I watch **extra film.** That's what makes me **a good leader. I don't cut any corners** to get to **where I am today."**

Bill Parcells (*Up Close Primetime, 1997*):

"There are **three things** you fight in pro sports every day. First, if you have **division from within,** you're losing. Okay? Then you're **fighting your direct competition** – in this case, it's the AFC East, okay? And then you're **fighting the media**. You have to fight it, because **the media can take your team out of control**."

Bobby Kersee, on what he's learned from his wife, Jackie Joyner-Kersee (*"Women & Sports at the Crossroads," Outside the Lines, 1997*):

{ "The female athlete is prepared mentally stronger than the male athlete. I know for a fact that Jackie, although maybe frightened of pain at times, can take more pain than I can." }

Tony Gwynn (*Up Close Primetime, 1996*):

"I LOVE THE FACT THAT I CAN GO UP TO THE PLATE AND DO THINGS RIGHT MORE TIMES THAN ANYBODY ELSE."

ABL point guard **Dawn Staley**, on wearing a rubber band on her wrist while playing (*ESPN.SportsZone, 1997*):

"I had heard that my favorite player of all time, Maurice Cheeks, snapped his wrist every time he made a turnover and I thought it would make a great disciplinary tool. In college, I was known as The Turnover Queen, but they weren't all my fault."

David Wells (*Up Close Primetime, 1997*):

"That first pitch is always the hardest because you're squeezing it: you don't want to throw a ball, you don't want to leave it down the middle, you want to get a strike and you hope that he misses it or he doesn't swing. It's the most intense pitch in baseball."

Randall Cunningham (*Sunday Conversation, 1995*):

"I've become a team player by sitting the bench."

Gary Sheffield's secret to hitting (*Up Close Primetime, 1997*):

"See it and hit it."

Bruce Jenner (*ESPN.SportsZone, 1996*):

"The **most challenging aspect** of the decathlon **is not the events themselves**, but **how you train** to become the **best 100-meter runner** you are on **the same day** that you're the **best 1,500-meter runner**."

Ken Griffey Jr. (*Up Close, 1993*):

"I can't play being mad. I go out there and have fun. It's a game, and that's how I am going to treat it."

Ernie Banks, on hitting a home run (*Up Close Primetime, 1996*):

"It's the feel of the ball **hitting** the **part of the bat** that is so **quiet**, so **soft**, so **gentle**, and **you know it's gone**. You just **feel it all the way to your toes** that it's gone."

Emmitt Smith (*Up Close Primetime, 1996*):

"Ninety percent of my success is behind the offensive line. Because as the line goes, I go."

"You create your own luck by the way you play. There is no such luck as bad luck. Fate has nothing to do with success or failure, because that is a negative philosophy that indicts one's confidence, and I'll have no part of it."

Greg Maddux, on his businesslike demeanor on the mound (*Up Close, 1996*):

"I really **expect to get guys out,** and when I do, **I don't want to act surprised.**"

Sonics coach **George Karl** (*SportsCenter, 1997*):

> ## "Momentum is as powerful as talent and Xs and Os a lot of the time."

Boxing promoter **Murad Muhammad,** on the lengths to which Don King will go ("*Tyson, the Return,*" *Outside the Lines, 1995*):

"He'll get **on his knees,** he'll get **naked,** he'll **crawl on the floor.** The name of the game is to **get the deal.**"

Pete Maravich (*Up Close, 1988*):

"I played six to 10 hours a day, every day, 90 days during the summer, and I'd do incredible things. I would dribble blindfolded in the house. I would take my basketball to bed with me, I'd lay there after my mother kissed and tucked me in, and I'd shoot the ball up in the air and say, Finger tip control, backspin, follow through."

Wade Boggs, on public opinion (*Sunday Conversation*, *1994*):

"Rod Carew told me in 1982 – and I have always remembered – for those who know you, no explanation is necessary. For those who don't, none is possible."

Karl Malone (*Up Close*, *1991*):

"When I went to college at Louisiana Tech, **Mom said do one thing**. Have people **love to see you coming**. Always. Don't have them mash your fingers **getting you out the door**. Have them **want you to stay**."

Julie Krone, accepting the ESPY for Outstanding Female Athlete (*ESPY Awards, 1993*):

"Our greatest glory is **not** in never failing, but in **rising every time we fall**."

Words of Wisdom

Lou Holtz (*Up Close, 1992*):

"There are **only three things** in this world about life: find something **you like to do**, find something **you do well** and find someone **to pay you to do it**."

Gary Player (*Up Close, 1997*):

"Get a good **education**, learn to **look after your body**, **eat right**, **dress properly**, and **try** and **behave well**."

Bill Walsh (*Up Close, 1991*):

"Whatever your job is, to think that you are good at it, among the best and, at some point, the very best is great gratification because you know you made a mark of some kind, however small, on mankind or your fellow neighbor."

Bobby Knight (*Up Close Primetime, 1996*):

"I've always felt that **the most important word** in the English language **is no**. You can **always change no to yes**, and that makes everybody feel good, but it's **hard to change yes to no**. I've always tried to tell kids that **if you're in doubt** about anything, **say no**."

Dale Brown (*Up Close, 1997*):

"John Wooden told me a long time ago, **Practice simplicity** with **constant repetition** and you'll **do all right** in your life."

"You've got to be on the verge of tears and laughter every day. Those people who keep their emotions inside, I feel sorry for. I cry easily and I laugh very easily. Opening ceremonies for the Olympics, I was crying my eyes out, holding hands with some plumber from Chicago."

The Soul of the Game

Announcer **Ernie Harwell**, on the National Pastime (*Up Close*, 1985):

"**BASEBALL** is **a spirited race** of man against man, reflex against reflex, **a game of inches** – every skill is measured, **every heroic act**, **every failing** is seen and cheered or booed and **then becomes a statistic**. In **BASEBALL**, **democracy shines** its clearest; the **only race** that matters is **the race to the bag**. The **creed is a rule book** and a color merely something **to distinguish a team's uniform** from another. **BASEBALL** is **a rookie**, his experience no bigger than the **lump in his throat** as he begins **fulfillment of his dreams**. It's **a veteran** too, a tired **old man** of 35 hoping that **those aching muscles** can pull him through **another sweltering** August and September."

"He is out there somewhere in spring training. He's probably 20 or 21, maybe 22. And he will retire in the year 2016. He will be the grand old man of baseball. And they will say, he's so old that the year he broke in, Eddie Murray was still playing. And he will become the ninth man. Eddie Murray's the eighth man. When he broke in, Brooks Robinson was still playing. And when Robinson broke in, Bob Feller was still playing. And when Feller broke in, Rogers Hornsby was still playing. And when Hornsby broke in, Honus Wagner was still playing. And when Wagner broke in, Cap Anson was still playing. And when Anson broke in, Dickey Pearce was still playing. And when Pearce broke in, Doc Adams was still playing. Adams played for the Knickerbocker club in the first organized game of baseball in 1846, number one of the eight men whose careers cover the 152 seasons since. And somewhere out there is the ninth man."

Floyd Patterson, on boxing (*"Boxing on the Ropes," Outside the Lines, 1993*):

"It's like being **in love** with a **woman**. She can be **faithful**, she can be **mean**, she can be **cruel**, but **if you love her**, you **want** her **even though** she can do you **all kinds of harm**."

Packer fan Randy Rutherford, on the Lambeau Leap (*"Inside Titletown U.S.A.," Outside the Lines, 1996*):

"In New York they **throw stuff at the players.** Here the **players throw themselves** at us."

Richard Petty, on racing (*Sunday Conversation, 1992*):

"**We do this for four** and a half **hours, no time-outs, no substitutes.** You use your **physical ability,** you use your **mental ability,** and if something happens they come out and **scrape you off the wall.**"

Jim Valvano, on college basketball (*Up Close, 1991*):

"Nobody's bigger than the game. The game is what it's all about. For me, it's vast – I'm in awe of it. We won a national championship, right? Still, there's not a gym I can walk into without wanting to go over and take a shot. Gotta take a j. I have a pretty good j, by the way."

Bob Ley, on collecting baseball cards (*"The Autograph Game," Outside the Lines, 1990*):

"We all remember the rush of anticipation opening a fresh pack of cards, the ritual of Got 'em, got 'em, need 'em, got 'em. It seemed to make summers last forever. A clothespin and a penny card turned a Schwinn into a Harley."

Tommy Lasorda, on the ups and down of managing the Dodgers (*Up Close, 1992*):

"All day long, I'm happy. When **I get to the ballpark,** I'm happy. When **the game begins,** I'm happy. For **six or seven innings** when **we're out in front,** I'm happy. Then **the last couple of innings** when **we lose,** I'm sad. Then **I'm sad the rest of the night**, and then **when I wake** up, **I'm happy again."**

Dick Vitale, on why he has the best job in the world (*Up Close, 1995*):

"In the last five days I've been at UCLA, I've been at Carolina, I've been at Duke, and I'm at Indiana on Tuesday. Who else sits courtside and gets paid for something they love? As long as my family and I are healthy, I have a fantasy life. If it ended tomorrow, it's been a trip to Disney World. Baby, it's been awesome!!!"

Jim Brown, on the Ryder Cup (*Up Close Primetime, 1995*):

"The **only true sport** in America **today** is the **Ryder Cup**, because it is simply about a **team winning**, where **true emotions** prevail, and people choke, and they **get exalted** and **it brings players together** like nothing else I've seen."

Willie "Pops" Stargell, on what he knows (*Up Close, 1993*):

"I know that **prayer** begins peace.
I know that **hard work** brings just rewards.
I know that **respect** creates gentlemen.
I know that **on a cold winter morning** in Pittsburgh, I enjoy a good bottle of Korbel Brut **champagne** with the **Sunday papers**.
I know that **good friends** and **good things** will **keep b.s. away**.
I know that **hitting a baseball**, especially a **home run**, is like a **runaway freight train** and the **first time** you have **sex**.
I know that rubbing shoulders with **good people**, **not great** people, is **a real joy**.
I know that **I know what I don't know**."

[*calling it a game*]

Shakespeare put it best: "Parting is such sweet sorrow." It hurts to leave. Whether we're separating from family, friends, a job or a team, we want to hang on for just one more minute. In the world of sports, the most feared enemy is time. Season by season, day by day, the body slowly gives in. One morning, you wake up and realize you can't run as fast, jump as high or heal as quickly as before. Resist all you want, fight as hard as you can, but time always wins. Eventually, even the greats of the game have to accept that their games are over. –LARRY BEIL

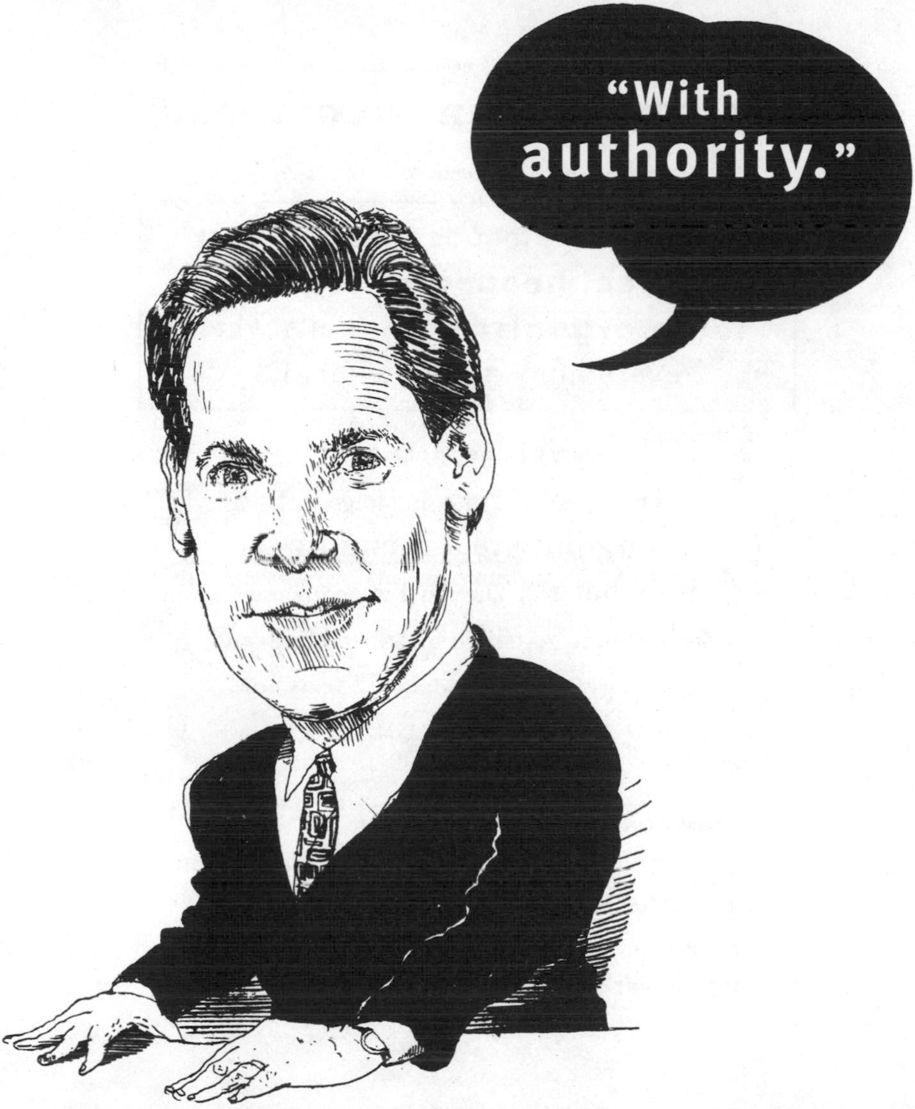
"With authority."

Robert Parish, announcing his retirement after 21 seasons (*Up Close, 1997*):

"My time has run out of time."

Lou Holtz, on retiring from Notre Dame (*Up Close, 1997*):

"Everybody's needed and, **if you don't feel needed or important to an organization**, that's when everything goes downhill."

Jimmy Connors (*Up Close, 1991*):

"Once I leave, I'm going to go with nothing but great memories and no what ifs. The day I wake up and I don't want to go out and work and train and love this game like I have for 25 years now, then it's time for me to go."

Tommy Lasorda, on retiring from the Dodgers (*Up Close, 1997*):

"In everybody's lifetime there will come a time when **one door will close on you**. If you're so concerned with the **one** that closes, you'll never find **the one that's open**."

Michael Jordan, on his retirement from the NBA (*Sunday Conversation, 1995*):

"I can walk away from the game and not worry about a lot of things that happened, the traveling, the stardom, the respect, the money. Those are all monetary things that don't mean much to me anyway. I play the game because I love the game. If I don't have a purpose, I walk away from the game."

Michael Jordan, on his decision to pursue a major league baseball career (*"Jordan's Dream Spring," Outside the Lines, 1994*):

"It's no gimmick. That's my motto: It was no gimmick from Day One."

Bobby Knight, on how he would like to be remembered (*Up Close Primetime, 1997*):

"As Abraham Lincoln once said, when it comes time for me to give up on the reins of this administration, if I have but one friend left, and that friend resides deep within me, then I'll be satisfied."

Magic Johnson, announcing his re-retirement (*ESPN Special Report, 1996*):

"I'm a **Laker.** I'm L.A. I'm an L.A. person. **I'm not going anywhere.** This is where I should end up and **this is where I'm ending my career.**"

Jim Kelly, on retiring from the Bills (*Sunday Conversation, 1997*):

"I've lost the desire to want to go out there each and every week and put my body on the line."

Carl Lewis, after the Atlanta Olympics (*Up Close, 1997*):

"After **I left the podium** in Atlanta, **I felt so fulfilled** in my career that **I lost my desire to compete** at that level again."

Bo Jackson, on the hip injury that forced his retirement (*SportsCenter, 1994*):

"God has his way of opening up our eyes to see reality. The way he opened my eyes is to allow me to have this hip injury. That is a rough way to go, but I had to accept the fact."

Kirby Puckett, speaking at Kirby Puckett Night at the Metrodome after his retirement (*SportsCenter, 1996*):

"Lou Gehrig stood in front of a packed house in Yankee Stadium, and I think I heard him say he thought he was the luckiest man in the world to be standing here. I'm just here to tell Lou Gehrig, Iron Horse, that tonight, Kirby Puckett is the luckiest man in the world."

Magic Johnson, on Larry Bird's retirement (*SportsCenter, 1993*):

"Larry Bird said, 'There will be another Larry Bird one day.' And **Larry, there will never, ever, ever** be another Larry Bird."

Terry Bradshaw's advice to Steve Young (*Up Close Primetime, 1997*):

"I tell you right here, brother, if you can play until they run you off, suit it up and you keep competing. If I could have done it, I would have done the same thing. I am so lucky that I was hurt. I had no choice."

Joe Montana to Bruce Smith, after the quarterback had to scramble several times during a game to avoid being sacked by the Bills defensive end (*Sunday Conversation*, *1994*):

"I'm **too old** for this ____."

"Mean" Joe Greene, on a surprise retirement present (*SportsCenter*, *1996*):
"Back in **1977** I got **tossed out** of a ball game for **slugging** a player and **I was** fined $5,000. **Two years after** I retired, I got a **check** in the **mail** for $5,000 **from Pete Rozelle** for **that fine.**"

Announcer **Harry Caray,** dismissing rumors he would retire (*Up Close*, *1996*):
"I've only **been doing it** for **52 years**. I think with some experience, I **might** get a **little bit better**."

Roy Williams, on Dean Smith's retirement (*SportsCenter*, *1997*):
"There's **not a single** North Carolina player or assistant coach who worked for him that makes **a major decision** in their life **without checking with Coach Smith,** and **that's a heck of a burden.**"

Deion Sanders, on his plans after sports (*Up Close, 1997*):

"My TESTIMONY in church this year – that
MEANT MORE to me than a Super Bowl or World Series
because THAT'S MY CALLING, man. I'm a pastor, I'M A
MINISTER and I will tear a church apart one day."

Marv Levy, on his reasons for retiring from the Bills (*SportsCenter, 1997*):

"The **depth of anguish** I felt **after every loss** over the **past few years** has begun to **reach an intensity** that the **thrill of victory couldn't overcome**."

Evander Holyfield, on how he'd like to be remembered (*Sunday Conversation, 1997*):

"As the man that was heavyweight champion of the world, but most importantly, as the man who touched a lot of people's lives, who motivated people to be the best that they could be, who gave a person a sense they could be a champion too if they are willing to pay the price that's necessary."

Brian Bosworth, on whether he's planning a comeback (*ESPN.SportsZone, 1997*):

"No. You have to be able to pass the physical."

Life After Sports

Mario Andretti, just prior to his retirement (*Sunday Conversation, 1994*):

"There should be **life after driving a race car** and **I hope I discover it**."

"Football is a very short-term proposition.
Football really prepares you for nothing.
The only thing I got out of football was
the ability to work hard, and that's it."

Panthers linebacker **Kevin Greene** (*Up Close Primetime, 1996*):

**"I don't know what I'm going
to do after football's over**. I'm
going to hide in the park someday
and sneak up on somebody when he's
drinking water out of the fountain,
**hit him in the back, and go,
CLIP-15 fifteen yards!,** and just
start walking off in any direction."

Jim Valvano (*Up Close, 1984*):

"The kids who play for me, I want them to
understand that **someday the cheering
stops**. They're not going to say, Now here he
comes, starting at left desk, give him a hand."

[*heroes*]

CHAPTER **16**

I can sum up how I feel in simple Vitale-ese: These performers are flat-out PTPers! Awesome, baby, with a capital A! Michael Jordan? His style, grace and class make him the greatest player ever to lace 'em up. Muhammad Ali? Simply the best. Not only unbelievable in the ring, but his unique charisma made him the darling of many. Jimmy Valvano? Wow! One of the best Cinderella stories in college basketball history, but his legacy for me will always be the determination he showed in his gallant battle with the Big C. I'll never forget his stimulating speech at the 1993 ESPY Awards, in which he inspired us to never give up, never *ever* give up in our own battles. –DICK VITALE

Jim Brown, on Muhammad Ali (*"Ali: Still the Greatest," Outside the Lines, 1994*):

{ "He defied everything. He defied the government. He defied white folks. He defied black folks. He defied everything." }

Don King, on Muhammad Ali (*Sunday Conversation, 1991*):

"Every knee must bend, every head must bow, every tongue must testify, thou art **The Greatest** of all time."

Billy Crystal, on Mickey Mantle (*SportsCenter, 1991*):

"He just was everything. If it was a hot, gorgeous day and I lived right on the beach, I'm inside watching the Yankees. **I limp like him.** I walk like him. At my Bar Mitzvah **I had an Oklahoma accent.** After my haftorah I wanted a beer. And I think I once told my parents, **Play me or trade me.**"

Magic Johnson, on Wayne Gretzky (*SportsCenter, 1996*):

"I've never seen a player outside of basketball about whom I said, **Man, he plays just like I do**. No-look passes, dropping them back. I mean, he was just a beautiful hockey player to watch. **He turned L.A. into a hockey town.** He was a celebrity among celebrities in a celebrity town."

Chris Berman, on Pete Rozelle (*NFL Countdown, 1996*):

"Football is in good hands because Pete Rozelle's hands were on it for so long. The games were talked about but rarely seen when he took office in 1960. When he left in 1989, it was a religion."

Alexi Lalas, on Pele (*ESPN.SportsZone, 1996*):

"He comes up to my nipple and yet, standing next to him, I feel like a dwarf. That's how big he is and what he's given the sport of soccer."

Hank Aaron, on what he would ask Babe Ruth (*Up Close Primetime, 1996*):

"I would ask him, **Were you proud of me?** And I'm sure the answer would be, **Yes, I was very proud of you, Hank.** I was glad of all the **records that you accomplished** and it couldn't have happened to **a nicer guy.**"

Howard Cosell, on Vince Lombardi (*Up Close, 1983*):

"The most **inspirational** football coach that has yet lived. A dead-honest, dead-moral man. **I loved him**."

Jack Nicklaus, on Arnold Palmer (*Up Close, 1991*):

"Arnold **related a lot to the people** and rightly so. **He brought a lot** of things **into the game of golf** that the golf game **needed.** It was a **spark**, it was a **boost**, and when you come and **beat the king,** people are **not going to be happy**."

Bob Costas, on Arthur Ashe (*Up Close, 1995*):

"Arthur Ashe was a singular individual. **He had an ability to be a pioneer.** Then you couple that with his **extraordinary personal virtues** and **qualities** and his **ability to be reflective** and **not simply react out of emotion**."

Bob Ley, on Mario Lemieux (*SportsCenter, 1993*):

{ "It's **rare** to link the words **hope** and **cancer** in the same phrase, and **Lemieux did it. And** he did it beautifully on ice, too." }

Reggie Jackson, on Ted Williams (*Up Close Primetime, 1996*):

"He's the Duke. John Wayne was the Duke,
but **he's the Duke for our game of baseball**. He's a
natural resource that we still have, and I cherish him."

John Saunders, on Jim Valvano (*SportsCenter, 1993*):

"He was a special person. And when I mean
special, I'm talking once in a lifetime."

Roberto Clemente's widow, **Vera**, on her husband's death
in 1972 while flying with supplies on a relief effort to Nicaragua
(*"Major League Béisbol," Outside the Lines, 1997*):

"The way he died was the way he lived –
always helping others."

Bob Ley, on Ken Griffey Jr. (*"Sports, Inc.," Outside the Lines, 1996*):

"Ken Griffey Jr. has exploded into a harmonic convergence
of once in a generation talent, epic moments and
a winning smile – just as his game badly needs it."

Ken Griffey Jr., on Cal Ripken Jr. (*Sunday Conversation, 1996*):

"He makes us all look bad."

Charley Steiner, on A.J. Foyt (*SportsCenter, 1994*):

"There are s**ome things** you can
rely on every year of your life. On
April 15th you pay your taxes, May 30th
or 31st A.J. Foyt is in the Indy 500.
Well, I'm still paying taxes."

ABC News chairman **Roone Arledge,** on Howard Cosell
(*"Howard Cosell: His Life and Times,"* Outside the Lines, *1991*):

"He's the garlic that makes the stew work."

Agent **David Falk,** on his client Michael Jordan (*Up Close, 1997*):

"There will never be another
Michael Jordan and there never should be.
If you can re-engineer all the things that make
Michael Michael, you'd need a lightning bolt
to strike the mixture and ignite it to create the
kind of magic that he has created."

Kevin McHale, on Larry Bird (*SportsCenter, 1993*):

"I'll tell you, when you play **second fiddle** to
Larry Bird, you still play a pretty **mean** fiddle
'cause Birdie was the best."

Roy Williams, on Dean Smith calling to console him after Kansas lost
to UNC in the NCAA tournament (*Up Close, 1997*):

"I've always said he was the best ever on the
court, but even better off the court."

Jackie Robinson

Jesse Jackson (*"Breaking the Line: Jackie Robinson's Legacy," Outside the Lines, 1997*):

"On that dash between birth and death
is where our lives are lived. On that dash many live
meaningless or meaningful lives.
Jackie, on that dash, emerged as an authentic
American and, indeed, global hero.

"On that dash, Jackie stole bases.
On that dash, he solved the pain of others.
On that dash, he swung the bat while pitchers
threw balls at his head. On that dash, Jackie bore the
burden and the scars of a people,
the destiny of a nation.

"And then, of course, 25 years after playing
baseball, Jackie made the dash home.
He stole home. The team won. America won.
Jackie won. Because God sent this very special
person our way to make us better."

Hank Aaron (*"Breaking the Line: Jackie Robinson's Legacy," Outside the Lines, 1997*):

"Jackie **passed the torch** to **every black player**. Now, whether that player **accepted it or not** was up to him."

Kansas City teammate **Buck O'Neill** (*"Breaking the Line: Jackie Robinson's Legacy," Outside the Lines, 1997*):

"You know what he did for us **more** than his playing baseball? He taught us that we were **as good** as anybody else, that we were spending **our money** and we **didn't have to take these things**. We never got gas at a filling station where we couldn't **go to the restroom**. We never played ball in a town that they didn't have **a place for us to stay**. We never played ball in a town that they didn't have **a place for us to eat. That was Jackie Robinson.**"

Spike Lee (*Up Close, 1990*):

"Besides Malcolm and Martin, I don't think there is any other black American who went through what Jackie did."

Howard Cosell (*Up Close, 1993*):

"The **most important friend** I ever had. The **greatest** influence in my life, **far more than a sports hero**, an American hero."

index

237